RENÉ GUÉNON: SOME OBSERVATIONS

FRITHJOF SCHUON

RENÉ
GUÉNON

SOME
OBSERVATIONS

SOPHIA PERENNIS

HILLSDALE NY

'René Guénon: some observations'
originally published in French as
'Quelques critiques' in
René Guénon: Les Dossiers H
© L'Age d'Homme 1984
All three articles © Courtesy of World Wisdom
Sophia Perennis 2004
All rights reserved

Series editor: James R. Wetmore

For information, address:
Sophia Perennis, P.O. Box 611
Hillsdale NY 12529
sophiaperennis.com

Library of Congress Cataloging-in-Publication Data

Schuon, Frithjof, 1907–1998
[Quelques critiques. English]
René Guénon : some observations / Frithjof Schuon.

p. cm.
Includes bibliographical references and index.
ISBN 0 900588 85 3 (alk. paper)
1. René Guénon I. Title.
B2430.G84 .S3413 2004
194—dc21   2004008278

CONTENTS

EDITORIAL NOTE

Chapter one, 'René Guénon: definitions', was published in *Études Traditionnelles* (Paris), July–November 1951, vol. 52, nos. 293, 294, 297, in *France-Asie* (Saigon), January 1953, 7th year, vol. 8, no. 80, and, in English, in *Sophia: A Journal of Traditional Studies*, vol. 1, no. 1, winter 1995. Chapter two, 'René Guénon: a note', first appeared in *René Guénon*, a compendium edited by Jean-Pierre Laurant (Paris: Les Editions de l'Herne, 1985), and, in English, in *Studies in Comparative Religion* (Bedfont, near London), vol. 17, nos. 1 and 2, winter/spring 1985 (as 'A Note on René Guénon'. Chapter three, 'René Guénon: some observations', was published in French as 'Quelques critiques' in *René Guénon: Les Dossiers H* (Lausanne: L'Âge d'Homme, 1984), a large volume of articles on René Guénon edited by Pierre-Marie Sigaud. The English translation was revised and edited by Mr Schuon himself shortly before he died. The appended article by Paul Sérant first appeared in *La Parisienne, Revue Littéraire Mensuelle*, March 1954, pp334–340, and the letter of April 16, 1946 was provided by Dr William Stoddart, courtesy of Mr Schuon's literary estate. It also appears in the compendium *René Guénon* mentioned above. We thank the executors of the literary estate of Frithjof Schuon for permission to print the materials under their control.

FOREWORD

René Guénon (1886–1951) and Frithjof Schuon (1907–1998) were the originators of what has subsequently become known as the 'traditionalist' or 'perennialist' school of wisdom. Guénon was the pioneer, and Schuon the fulfillment. Other wisdom schools with dual originators and expositors are those associated with Socrates and Plato in fifth-century Athens, and with Jalāl ad-Dīn Rūmī and Shams ad-Dīn at-Tabrīzī in thirteenth-century Turkey.

Guénon and Schuon were philosophers of a wholly traditional kind, inspired first and foremost by the Vedantic doctrine of *advaita* (non-duality), especially as expressed by the Hindu sage Shankara. In another sense, they could be said to be philosophers in the tradition of Pythagoras, Socrates, and Plato, and also of the Medieval Scholastics. From their point of view, Western philosophy ended with the Middle Ages, and 'thinkers' thereafter—such as Descartes (1596–1659) and Kant (1724–1804) and those following—would have to be designated by another term. The cleavage is deep: the starting-point of the Greek and Medieval philosophers ('lovers of wisdom') was certainty, whereas the starting-point of the modern philosophers is doubt.

Guénon traced the origin of what he called the modern deviation to the arrival of the Renaissance, that cataclysmic inrush of secularization, when nominalism vanquished realism, individualism (or humanism) replaced universalism, and empiricism banished scholasticism. An important part of Guénon's work was therefore his critique of the modern world from an implacably 'Platonic' or metaphysical point of view. This was fully expounded in his two masterly volumes, *The Crisis of the Modern World* and *The Reign of Quantity*. The positive side of Guénon's work was his exposition of the immutable principles of universal metaphysics and traditional orthodoxy. As mentioned, his primary source was the Shankaran doctrine of 'non-duality', and his chief work in this respect is *Man and His Becoming according to the Vedānta*. However, he also turned readily to other traditional sources, since he considered all traditional forms to be various expressions of the one supra-formal Truth. A final aspect of Guénon's work was his brilliant exposition of the intellectual content of traditional symbols, from whichever religion they might come. See in this connection his *Science of Sacred Symbols*.

It is important to note that Guénon's writings, decisively important though they were, were purely 'theoretical' in character, and made no pretense of dealing with the question of realization. In other words, they were generally concerned with intellectuality (or doctrine) and not directly with spirituality (or method).

The sun rose for the traditionalist school with the appearance of the work of Frithjof Schuon (1907–1998). Thirty years ago, an English Thomist, Bernard Kelly, wrote of him: 'His work has the intrinsic authority of a contemplative intelligence.' More recently, a senior American academic, Professor Huston Smith declared: 'In depth and breadth, a paragon of our time. I know of no living thinker who begins to rival him.' T. S. Eliot's perception was similar. Regarding Schuon's first book, he wrote in 1953: 'I have met with no more impressive work in the comparative study of Oriental and Occidental religion.'

Guénon and Schuon corresponded over a period of many years, and Schuon paid two visits to Guénon in Cairo in the late 1930s. Until his dying day, Guénon, following an Arab practice, addressed Schuon in his correspondence as 'my dear brother' and, in the pages of *Études Traditionnelles*, as 'our eminent collaborator'.

Schuon's work began to appear during the latter part of Guénon's life, and he continued, in even more notable fashion, Guénon's perspicacious and irrefutable critique of the modern world, reaching unsurpassable heights in his exposition of the essential truth—illuminating and saving—that lies at the heart of every revealed form. Schuon called this supra-formal truth the *religio perennis*. This term, which does not imply a rejection of the similar terms *philosophia perennis* and *sophia perennis*, nevertheless contains a hint of an additional dimension which is unfailingly present in

Schuon's writings. This is that intellectual understanding entails a spiritual responsibility, that intelligence requires to be complemented by sincerity and faith, and that 'seeing' (in height) implies 'believing' (in depth). In other words, the greater our perception of essential and saving truth, the greater our obligation towards an effort of inward or spiritual 'realization'.

Schuon, who acquired a knowledge of French as a child, wrote more than two dozen books in that language, all of them translated into English. His first work was a comprehensive general study, the very title of which serves to set the scene: *The Transcendent Unity of Religions*. Further works include: *Language of the Self* (on Hinduism), *Treasures of Buddhism*, *Understanding Islam*, *Castes and Races*, *Logic and Transcendence*, and a wide-ranging compendium of philosophic and spiritual enlightenment entitled *Esoterism as Principle and as Way*. Though none of his books deals exclusively with Christianity, many of them contain systematic treatments of the main Christian themes, above all the doctrine of the Trinity. In the years immediately preceding his death, he composed a long cycle of didactic and lyrical poems (over three thousand in all) in his native German. A selection of one hundred of these has been published in a bilingual German-English edition entitled *Songs for a Spiritual Traveler*. He also wrote *Road to the Heart*, a book of poems in English. His last three books were in a sense the apotheosis of his writing career. They are: *Roots of the Human Condition*, *The Play of Masks*, and *The Transfiguration of Man*.

Guénon and Schuon were concerned with the Total Truth, and their doctrinal expositions were based on *intellectus purus*. Their main theses include the fundamental and essential principles of universal metaphysics (with its cosmological and anthropological ramifications), intellectual intuition, orthodoxy, tradition, universality, the science of symbolism; spirituality in the broadest sense; esthetics and the meaning and importance of sacred art; intrinsic morality. As mentioned above, a very important characteristic is their deep-reaching critique of the modern world, on the basis of strictly traditional principles.

This perennialist current of intellectuality and spirituality has and may well be called 'a phenomenon of our time,' but unlike other contemporary phenomena, it remains largely a secret one, a 'still small voice', a hidden presence, sought out only by those with a hunger and thirst for it, and known only to those with eyes to see and ears to hear.

In all of this, Guénon was a pioneer. Before him, no one in modern times had expounded the principles of truth and intellectuality in such a complete and uncompromising manner; and above all, no one had perceived and defined the errors and deviations of the modern world with such perspicacity and philosophical clarity. Nevertheless, in plowing this furrow, Guénon was completely alone, and it was probably his isolation, coupled with his uncompromising nature, that led him occasionally to commit certain infelicities in his analysis and in his writings. It is in regard to these that Schuon performs an outstanding service, by delineating and correcting certain shortcomings, while at the same time recognizing, and offering to our view, Guénon's unquestioned greatness. In his critique, Schuon puts into effect one of Guénon's own principles: one must put everything in its proper place.

A remarkable gift of Schuon's is that, when he undertakes to 'criticize' someone of value, the reader ends up (not only because of the power, but also because of the charity, of what he says) by having an even higher esteem for the one criticized that ever before! Cases in point are St John of the Cross and René Guénon. In the case of the first, one is enabled positively to 'feel' his sanctity; and in the case of the second, one acquires a blindingly clear idea of his great gifts, and of his pioneer-like and pivotal role.

WILLIAM STODDART

1

RENÉ GUÉNON:
DEFINITIONS

THE WORK OF RENÉ GUÉNON may be defined by four words: intellectuality, universality, tradition, theory.

The work is 'intellectual' because it concerns knowledge and because it envisages this in conformity with its nature, namely, in the light of the intellect, which is essentially supra-rational. It is 'universal' inasmuch as it views the different Revelations in terms of the one Truth, while adopting, as the occasion demands, the language of a particular tradition. Moreover, the work of Guénon is 'traditional' because the fundamental facts that it conveys are strictly in conformity with the teaching of the great traditions, or with one of these traditions when it is a case of one form amongst others. Finally, the work is 'theoretical' since it does not directly envisage spiritual realization, and it even refrains from assuming the role of a practical teaching, and from placing itself, for example, on the grounds of the teachings of a Ramakrishna.

This brings us to the question of content: it converges essentially on metaphysical doctrine—not on what may be called 'spiritual life'—and is subdivided into four great subjects: metaphysical doctrine, traditional principles, symbolism, criticism of the modern world.

❖

LET US SPEAK FIRST of metaphysical doctrine. Here, the merit of Guénon is not simply to have expounded it, but above all to have explained its true nature, by distinguishing it clearly from 'philoso-phies' in the current meaning of this term; this meaning, while doubtless not exclusive, at any rate marks a strong predominance of ratiocination over intellectual intuition, to the point of reducing the latter to a sort of more or less unconscious 'accident'. Herein lies the great merit of the Guénonian thesis: to have recalled what mod-ern thought, in the manner of 'classical' thought, has forgotten or sought to forget, namely the essential distinction between intellec-tual intuition and mental operation or, in other words, between the Intellect, which is universal, and the reason, which is individual and even specifically human. And this cuts short all speculations lacking any transcendent character; indeed, to reach Truth, one must awa-ken in oneself—if this be possible—the intellective faculty, and not try to 'explain' by means of reason realities which one does not 'see'; most philosophies start from a sort of axiomatic blindness, whence their hypotheses, their calculations, their conclusions, all of which are unknown in pure metaphysics, the dialectic of the latter being based on analogy and symbolism.

Basically, metaphysical doctrine is nothing other than the science of Reality and illusion, and it presents itself, from the starting-point of the terrestrial state—and thus with its cosmological extension—as the science of the existential or principial degrees, as the case may be: on the one hand it, distinguishes within the Principle itself between Being and Non-Being, or in other words between the personal God and the impersonal Divinity; on the other hand, within Manifestation, metaphysics—now become cosmology—dis-tinguishes between the formless and the formal, the latter being in turn divided into two states, the one subtle or animic and the other gross or corporeal.

The second great subject treated by Guénon is tradition, or more precisely the aggregate of principles that constitute it, whatever its form; we can say that tradition is whatever joins all that is human to Divine Truth. Guénon emphasizes, not only the distinction between what is traditional and what is not, but also, on the level of tradition itself, the distinction between the two fundamental aspects of tradition, namely exoterism and esoterism, the latter directly rejoining metaphysical doctrine.

As for symbolism, the third great subject of the Guénonian work, this is necessary because the natural and universal expression of metaphysics is the symbol. This expression is natural, because it resides in the nature of things, in other words, in real analogies, and it is universal in that it is capable of unlimited applications in the order of the Real. Symbolism has two advantages over ratiocination: first, far from artificially opposing what it expresses, it is in fact an aspect or an 'incarnation' of it; second, instead of suggesting merely one aspect of a given reality, it manifests several of them at the same time and presents truths in their various metaphysical and spiritual connections, thus opening up incommensurable 'dimensions' to contemplation.

Finally, as fourth great subject, the Guénonian work includes the criticism of the modern world; it cannot but include it, given on the one hand its intellectual and traditional character, and on the other hand its sphere of action which is precisely this world deprived of intellectuality and tradition as determining factors. This critique of modernism is presented under two aspects, one general and the other detailed; in other words, the author criticizes on the one hand the specific tendencies of the civilization in which we live, and on the other detailed expressions of this civilization, for example, the different forms of 'neo-spiritualism'.

❖

LIKE ALL WORKS OF AN EXCEPTIONAL BREADTH, that of René Guénon can give rise to different interpretations, not with regard to its overall truth, but with regard to its nature and its application. In our opinion, the role of René Guénon was to state principles rather than show how to apply them: it is in the enunciation of fundamental principles that his intellectual genius is exercised with an incontestable mastery; but that one should accept without reservation all the examples and all the deductions that the author proffers to us throughout his numerous writings, would seem to us to be a question of opinion, or even of faith, especially as the knowledge of the facts depends on contingencies which cannot intervene in principial knowledge. If the Intellect is so to speak sovereign and infallible on its own terrain, it can only exercise its discernment on the plane of facts in a conditional manner; moreover, God can intervene on this plane with particular and sometimes unpredictable wishes, of which principial knowledge can only take account *a posteriori*. The plane of facts is in some respects the opposite of that of principles, in the sense that it comprises modalities and imponderables which are at the opposite extreme from the wholly 'mathematical' rigor of universal laws; at least it is so in appearance, for it goes without saying that universal principles do not contradict one another; even under the veil of the inexhaustible diversity of the possible, their immutability is always discernible, provided that the intelligence be in the conditions necessary to discern it. This means that 'intellectual intuition' may depend on very complex factors which sometimes seem to have no connection with the realities which the intelligence proposes to understand.

It would be rendering poor service to the truths of which René Guénon chose to be the interpreter to dissimulate what in his work may be a stumbling block for some and a source of confusion for others, as experience has shown us; without wishing to go into detail, we shall restrict ourselves to mentioning the following: to the extent that the words 'intellectuality' and 'spirituality' are applicable to different realities, one can say that the Guénonian work is 'intellectual' and that it is best not to look in it for anything but 'ideas'; moreover, one ought not to confuse the particular 'temperament' of the author with the East, nor with the traditional mentality in general. We would add here that one may find surprising, as Coomaraswamy does, the sometimes excessive exclusivism of Guénon's terminology; this trait is doubtless analogous to the rather 'mathematical'—and not 'visual'—character of Guénon's thought, as regards, not the intellectual content, but the mode of operation.

Now if, on the doctrinal plane, Guénon's work is of a unique kind, it is perhaps important to specify that this does not stem from a more or less 'prophetic' nature, a proposition which Guénon himself already rejected in advance, but from an exceptional cyclical conjuncture of circumstances, whose temporal aspect is this 'end of a world' in which we live, and whose spatial aspect—as a function, moreover, of the cyclical aspect—is the forced bringing together of the different civilizations; it can thus be said that for the West, Guénon is the providential interpreter of this conjuncture, at least on the level of doctrine; we say 'interpreter', but we might also add 'victim', in the sense that this role demanded 'unilateral' or 'disproportionate' activities and experiences which did not occur without leaving profound traces in the man and his writings. Be that as it may, such a work would have been without object in a period such as the Middle Ages, because the 'end of a world' was still too far off and wisdom was not neglected as it is today as a result of modern tendencies; in addition, the spiritual perspectives of Asia were practically non-existent for Medieval Europe.

The modes of participation in Guénon's work are necessarily diverse: some readers have been influenced by it in a more or less partial or superficial manner, whereas others have been convinced by the very essence of the work; some have been 'converted' from the current errors of our time; others still, not in need of 'conversion', have found in Guénon what they already thought themselves, except for metaphysics which no one can draw forth from himself, and which they received from Guénon—apart from other possible, but in practice not sufficiently explicit, sources—as Guénon himself received it from the East, and as every Easterner receives it from another Easterner. At any rate, Guénon's role consists essentially in a function of transmission and commentary and not of inspired readaptation: 'I have no other merit,' he wrote to us in a letter, 'than to have expressed some traditional ideas to the best of my ability.' If this definition is indeed too modest in that it makes no mention of the speculative element in Guénon's work nor of the fundamental nature of the ideas he expounded, it nonetheless shows its intention and its nature.

2

RENÉ GUÉNON: A NOTE

IT HAS BEEN ASKED why Guénon 'chose the Islamic way' and not another; the 'material' answer is precisely that he did not have a choice, given that he did not accept the initiatic character of the Christian sacraments and that Hindu initiation was closed to him because of the caste system; given also that at the time concerned he considered Buddhism to be a heterodoxy. The key to the problem is that Guénon was seeking an initiation and nothing else; Islam offered him this, with all the essential and secondary elements that must normally accompany it. Also, it is not at all certain that Guénon would have entered Islam if he had not settled in a Muslim country; for he had received an Islamic initiation, through the intermediary of Abdul-Hādī, while he was still in France, and at that time he did not dream of practicing the Muslim religion. When he accepted the Shādhilī initiation, it was thus an initiation that Guénon chose, and not a 'way'.

Nevertheless, in Guénon's case there is something inadequate, troubling, and ill-sounding in the expression 'choosing a way'; for Guénon was intrinsically a 'pneumatic' of the 'gnostic' or jñānic type—and in this case the question of a 'way' does not arise, or at least changes its meaning so much that the very expression leads to confusion. The pneumatic is in a way the 'incarnation' of a spiritual archetype, which means that he is born with a state of knowledge which, for others, would be precisely the end and not the point of departure; the pneumatic does not 'progress' to something 'other than himself', he remains in place so as to become fully himself—namely his archetype—by progressively eliminating veils or husks, impediments contracted from the ambience and possibly also from heredity. He eliminates them by means of ritual supports—'sacraments', if one will—without forgetting meditation and prayer; but his situation is nevertheless quite different from that of ordinary men, even if they be prodigiously gifted. From another point of view, one should know that the born gnostic is by nature more or less independent, not only with regard to the 'letter', but also with regard to the 'law'; and this does not make for easy relations with his ambience, either psychologically or socially.

One must reply here to the following objection: does not the 'way', for all men, consist in eliminating obstacles and 'becoming oneself'? Yes and no; in other words, it is so metaphysically, but not humanly; for, I repeat, the pneumatic 'realizes' or 'actualizes' what he 'is', while the non-pneumatic realizes what he 'must become'—a difference which is both 'absolute' and 'relative', and which could be discussed indefinitely.

Another objection—or question—is the following: how can one explain the imperfections and gaps—which are indeed surprising—in Guénon's work, given the substantial quality of the author? But these gaps, precisely, were not at all of a kind that opposed this quality; they were so to speak 'accidental' and 'superimposed' and were certainly in no wise passional or worldly. They were rather hypertrophies or asymmetries, and in part traumatisms, reinforced by the absence of compensatory factors in his soul and his ambience.

One may nevertheless wonder why Providence permitted in Guénon's work shortcomings that seem incompatible with the profound personality of the author; the answer is that Providence would never have permitted—one may say so without temerity—a Guénonian opus that had no positive result; we are thinking here of an influence that is felt in the most diverse sectors, and this is the least that one can say. Guénon was the victim of a certain fatality, but his essential message was not in vain and could not be so, and this is all that matters.

Guénon was like the personification, not of spirituality as such, but uniquely of metaphysical certainty; or of metaphysical self-evidence in mathematical mode, which explains the abstract and mathematical nature of his doctrine, and also—indirectly and having in mind the absence of compensatory factors—certain traits of character. No doubt he had the right to be 'one-sided', but this constitution did not go well with the wide scope of his mission; he was neither a psychologist nor an esthete—in the best sense of these terms—in other words, he underestimated esthetic and moral values, especially in relation to their spiritual functions. He had an inborn aversion to anything that is human and 'individual', and this even affected his metaphysics in certain places, for example, when he thinks that he has to deny that the 'human state' enjoys a 'privileged' position, or that the 'mental element'—the essence of which is reason—constitutes a privilege for man; whereas in reality the presence of the rational faculty proves precisely the 'central' and 'total' character of the human state which would not exist without this character, which is its whole raison d'être.

Be that as it may, in mentioning these shortcomings, one must never forget two things: the irreplaceable value of what constitutes the essence of Guénon's work, and the gnostic or pneumatic substance of the author.

Guénon was entirely right in specifying that *Vedānta* is the most direct and, in a certain respect, the most assimilable expression of pure metaphysics; no attachment to any non-Hindu tradition obliges us not to know this, or to pretend not to know it. There is, on the part of the monotheistic Semitic religions, a *de facto* esoterism and a *de jure* esoterism; it is the latter—whether or nor it is recognized for what it is—that is the equivalent of Vedantic wisdom; the *de facto* esoterism is the one which derives from what has in fact been said or written, possibly with the concealment and side-tracking demanded by a given theological framework, and especially by a given religious *upāya*. It was no doubt esoterism *de jure* that the Kabbalists had in mind when they said that, if the esoteric tradition were lost, the sages could reconstitute it.

I have more than once had occasion to remark that esoterism has two aspects, one prolonging the respective exoterism and the other being foreign to it to the point of sometimes opposing it; for while it is true that the form in a certain way 'is' the essence, the essence for its part is in no wise the form; the drop is water, but water is not the drop. 'Only error is transmitted,' said Lao Tzu; likewise Guénon did not hesitate to write in the journal *La Gnose* that the historical religions are 'so many heresies' in relation to the 'primordial and unanimous Tradition', and he specifies in *The King of the World* that

> true esoterism is something quite different from outward religion and, if it has some relationships with it, this can only be in so far as it finds in the religious forms a mode of symbolical expression; it matters little, moreover, that these forms should be those of a particular religion. . . .

Guénon speaks of 'true esoterism', thereby admitting the existence of a mitigated esoterism, and this is what I mean when, in certain of my books, I speak of 'average Sufism'; a rather approximative expression, but in practice sufficient.

Let us now return to the question of the 'pneumatic', independently of any personal application: the quality of the born gnostic comprises not only modes, but also degrees; on the one hand there is the difference between the *jñānī* and the *bhakta*, and on the other there are differences of plenitude or scope in the manifestation of the archetype. At any rate, the pneumatic is situated, by his very nature, under the vertical and timeless axis—there is neither 'before' nor 'after'—so that the archetype which he personifies or 'incarnates', and which is truly 'himself' or 'itself', may at any moment pierce the contingent individual envelope: whence, in some—but not all—pneumatics, spiritual expressions which may seem excessive and cause scandal; but it is then the archetype that speaks through the envelope; it is therefore really 'himself' that speaks. The true gnostic does not attribute to himself any 'state', because he is without ambition and without ostentation; rather he has a tendency—from an 'instinct of self-preservation'—to dissimulate his nature, all the more so because he is obviously aware of the 'cosmic play' (*līlā*) and because it is difficult for him to take seriously what is serious for profane and worldly people; in other words, 'horizontal' beings who have no doubts about anything and who, like the 'humanists' they are, remain below the vocation of man.

What the born gnostic seeks, with regard to 'realization', is much less a 'way' than a 'framework'; a traditional, sacramental, and liturgical framework which will permit him to be more and more authentically 'himself', namely a particular archetype of the celestial 'iconostasis'. This brings to mind of the sacred art of India and the Far East, which demonstrates in a supernaturally evocative fashion the celestial models of earthly spirituality; this, precisely, is the raison d'être of this art which is both 'mathematical' and 'musical', and is founded on the principle of *darshan*, the visible and intuitive assimilation of the symbol-sacrament. This symbol, moreover, does not only apply to art, but also arises—and *a priori*—from animate and inanimate nature, for there is in all beauty a liberating, and ultimately saving, element; and this permits us this esoteric paraphrase: 'Whoever has eyes to see, let him see!'

'Know thyself,' said the inscription above the portal of the Temple of Delphi; in other words, know thine immortal essence, but also, and thereby: know thine archetype. No doubt this injunction applies in principle to all men, but it applies to the pneumatic in a much more direct manner, in the sense that, by definition, he is aware of his celestial model, and this in spite of the shortcomings which his earthly husk may have undergone in contact with a too discordant ambience. Paradox is part of the economy of this low world, given that the limitlessness of universal Possibility necessarily implies unexpected, not to say incomprehensible, combinations; phenomena may be what they are, but *vincit omnia Veritas*.

3

RENÉ GUÉNON:
SOME OBSERVATIONS

*The following critical comments are based on personal
notes written many years ago. They were not originally
intended for publication, but there would now seem to
be no reason for keeping them private any longer.*

GUÉNON HAS RENDERED US an inestimable service in presenting
and expounding the crucial ideas of metaphysical science and pure
intellectuality, of integral tradition and traditional orthodoxy, of
symbolism and esoterism; and then in defining and condemning,
with implacable realism, the modern aberration in all its forms. But
this conspicuous merit should not prevent us—since 'there is no
right superior to that of truth'—from recognizing the often strange
faults which Guénon's works include; to point them out is not to
fail to appreciate the author's merits; on the contrary, it is to protect
the essential content of the message and, in a certain way, to protect
Guénon from himself.

❖

OF THE HINDU DOCTRINE of cosmic cycles, Guénon seems to
know only the following version: the four *Yugas* form a *Manvantara*; fourteen *Manvantaras* form a *Kalpa*, that is to say the 'total
development of a world.' Now according to the *Mānava-Dharma-
Shāstra* and several *Purānas*, the four *Yugas* form a *Mahāyuga*; a
thousand *Mahāyugas* form a *Kalpa*; seventy-one *Mahāyugas* form a

Manvantara, and fourteen *Manvantaras* form a *Kalpa,* which thus is equivalent to a thousand *Mahāyugas.* In not one of Guénon's writings is there the slightest allusion to this Puranic doctrine of the cycles which is nevertheless too important to leave unmentioned.

Guénon all too readily gives the appearance of an unlimited knowledge and indulges in outbursts like the following: 'This leads us to speak of the undue importance which, in the West, is customarily attributed to Buddhism: orientalists, because they are a little less ill acquainted with it than they are with other subjects, wish to see it everywhere, even where there is not the least trace of it.' Now Guénon knew infinitely less about Buddhism than the least of the orientalists; but let us continue the quotation from *Introduction to the Study of the Hindu Doctrines:*

> Obviously, when one encounters something with which one is not familiar, but which one knows to be of Eastern origin, one can always deal with the matter by declaring it to be Buddhist. Let it not be thought that we exaggerate; for there is no need to look very far to find, among other singularities, the *Kwan-yin* of Taoism transmuted into a *Bodhisattva!* 'Official' orientalists apply themselves all the more readily to this bizarre work of classification, intended to hide their more or less conscious embarrassment. . . .

What Guénon obviously did not know is that it is the Chinese themselves who identify *Kwan-Yin* with the Bodhisattva *Avalokiteshvara!* Be that as it may,

> Orientalists by virtue of the effective monopoly which they have succeeded in establishing to their profit, can be almost certain that no one is going to contradict them: what need those people fear who establish as a principle that there is no real competence . . . except such as is to be acquired at their own school.

So there it is!

❖

WHEN, in 'Magic and Mysticism',[1] Guénon describes mystics by remarking upon their 'passivity' and comparing them, in other respects, to magicians—which one notes with amazement—one does not know of what he can be speaking; and one knows no better on being informed later that Joan of Arc and Saint Bernard were not mystics but that Saint John of the Cross was; and if Saint John of the Cross was a mystic, one does not see why such and such a Sufi who resembles him is not one also, apart from the usual question-begging about 'initiation' as opposed to 'mysticism'.

One of the most astonishing things is Guénon's own astonishment over points which any child should understand. Thus, he is astonished at the 'exaltation of suffering' in Christianity, and he asks himself if this feature—'the causes of which it would be interesting to investigate'!—has not been 'superimposed on Christianity by the Western mentality. . . .' One would think that he had never heard either of the Passion or of the martyrs.

In his article on conversions, Guénon tells us that converts 'are not very interesting,' and he considers that 'the converter and the converted give proof of a like incomprehension concerning the profound meaning of their traditions.' 'Go and preach to all nations,' said Christ; he did not dream of forbidding proselytism or of belittling those who were converted. It is completely illogical to accept the existence of exoterism, which is willed by God, while not accepting that of exoterists, that is to say those limited to exoterism and capable, in consequence, of converting from one religion to another.

According to Guénon, to say that there are trials in life can only be an 'abuse of language, the origin of which, moreover, it would be interesting to investigate'; the only 'trials' worthy of the name are 'initiatic trials', which have the signal distinction of being rites and not experiences of 'profane' life! Now, all the sacred scriptures speak of the trials of life: to suffer a trial is to be purified, and it is, at the

---

1. *Perspectives on Initiation* (Hillsdale: Sophia Perennis, 2004), chap. 2.

same time, to prove whether one really believes what one is meant
to believe; for a living faith in God confers patience and trust. To
suffer heroically in God is without interest because it is profane; but
to take some steps on a carpet inlaid with symbols in a Masonic
Lodge, *there* is something interesting! And this is typical: for the
sake of refuting the ordinary conception of a trial, Guénon ascribes
to it an intention of pseudo-initiatic facility which no one else has
ever dreamt of, and thus transforms, as in his text on the
sacraments, his argument into a tilting at windmills.

❖

MORE THAN ONCE, one has the impression that Guénon reads into
documents what he wishes to find in them. For Dante, 'it is evident
that the temporal authority of the monarch devolves upon him
from the universal source of authority, without any intermediary';
this is the thesis of his treatise on monarchy; the emperor does not
receive his authority from the pope. But Guénon on the contrary
deems that

> the emperors themselves,...led astray by the extent of the
> power conferred on them, were the first to contest their sub-
> ordination vis-à-vis the spiritual authority, from whom, never-
> theless, they derived their power just like other sovereigns, but
> even more directly so.

And he then adds in a footnote: 'The Holy Empire begins with
Charlemagne, and it is known that it was the pope who conferred
upon him the imperial dignity....' But, according to Dante, it is not
the pope who confers on the emperor his authority; in fact he does
no more than consecrate him. This thesis of Dante's does not
prevent Guénon from citing its author at length on the subject of
the respective attributions of pope and emperor, and from adding
this:

> it is rather astonishing... that he who wrote these lines [namely
> Dante] could sometimes have been presented as an enemy of

the Papacy; no doubt ... he denounced the inadequacies and imperfections which he could see in the state of the papacy in his day.

All that is indeed rather astonishing! Besides: if the emperors could be 'led astray by the extent of the power conferred upon them'—which is precisely what Dante denies—the function of emperor would be without legitimacy and humanly unrealizable; now the attitude of the emperors did not in reality derive from their power, but solely from a point of principle, hence of doctrine, and not of morality. Furthermore, it seems to me that the emperors 'contested their subordination,' not 'vis-à-vis the spiritual authority' as such, but vis-à-vis what they looked upon as the papacy's abuses of power; for the pope and bishops were theoretically and practically princes, and therefore political authorities, and this by virtue of the Donation of Constantine which, for Dante, was contrary to the nature of things and consequently illegitimate. Dante did not confine himself to 'denouncing the inadequacies ... which he could see in the state of papacy in his day'; he denounced an entire aspect of the traditional papacy, namely the Constantinian aspect; and it is a truism to add that Dante was not an 'enemy of the papacy,' if by that is understood an enemy of pontifical authority.

For Dante, the authority of the pope comes from Christ and the authority of the emperor from natural law; so the pope cannot transfer his authority to the emperor any more than the emperor can transfer his authority to the pope, nor can either one have any right to the other's authority. 'He who can do the greater can do the lesser,' it will be objected from the Guelph side; but this truth is only applicable to the pontiffs in a relative way and in respect of their sacerdotal competence, otherwise there would be no princes. 'My kingdom is not of this world,' said Christ, and 'render unto Caesar the things that are Caesar's'; which implies that the pope's kingdom is not of this world, any more than is Christ's, and that he should not lay claim to what is rightfully due to the emperor.

❖

THERE IS, on the part of Guénon, a strange confusion between containers and contents: for example, he asserts that the word 'ideal' signifies nothing because everyone can suppose it to mean just about anything; one might as well say that the word 'animal' signifies nothing because it can be understood in relation to any species at all, and so on. Or let us take the assertion that Hinduism is not a 'religion' because it is not composed of the three elements 'dogma, morality, cult': apart from the fact that these elements are necessarily to be found in it after a certain fashion, Hinduism is quite obviously a religion, seeing that it is concerned with realities that are both metaphysical and eschatological. What is typical for Guénon is to prefer to say that Hinduism is not a religion rather than to say that it is a religion of a different kind.

And likewise: nothing is clearer than the notions of the 'subjective' and the 'objective' but, for Guénon, these 'present serious drawbacks from the point of view of clarity' because one can attribute anything whatsoever either to the side of the subjective or the side of the objective!

There is a Guénon who boldly plunges into Non-Being, and there is another who seems not to know how to count up to three; I think this paradox is not without significance, and it is even a key to many things. Too often, our author allows himself strangely weak arguments: for example, when he reproaches modern mathematicians with 'not knowing what number is,' confusing number with the written character, and 'using, in their notation, symbols whose meaning they no longer understand,' as though these things had any connection whatever with what legitimately concerns mathematicians; or when he reproaches Pascal for having defined space as 'a sphere whose center is everywhere and whose periphery is nowhere'—which is excellent when one understands its meaning— and for having spoken of two 'infinities' instead of accepting *a priori* that the word 'infinite' can only have an absolute and metaphysical sense; or when he reproaches modern men for having a quantitative notion of money, which means absolutely nothing—quite apart from the fact that quantity also has its right to existence and that it is precisely quantity which is the *raison d'être* of money; or when he asserts that the inhabitants of other planets would be quasi-invisible for us on account of their completely different sensations, for which I do not see the shadow of a justification since, like us, they exist in matter and since we are capable of perceiving even the Andromeda nebula; if they do not exist in matter the question does not arise and there is no reason to speculate on their faculties of sensation.

In *Man and His Becoming according to the Vedānta*, we read that the waking state possesses a 'relative reality and a stability sufficient to serve the needs of ordinary, profane life,' but that its difference with regard to the dream state 'does not imply an effective superiority of the waking state over the dream state when each is considered in itself,' and that a 'superiority which is valid only from a "profane" point of view cannot, metaphysically, be accounted a true superiority'! And Guénon even takes care to add that the 'possibilities of the dream state are more extensive than those of the waking state,' because 'they allow the individual to escape, in a cer-tain measure, from some of the limiting conditions to which he is subject in his corporeal modality'! So, whether a saint dreams of being a criminal, or a criminal dreams of being a saint, it is 'meta-physically' equivalent, and the criminal's dream is even superior to the waking reality of the saint if the malefactor dreams of floating in the air without, moreover, having the option of dreaming anything else!

Or again: for Guénon the notion of 'matter' is factitious, con-fused, problematic; it has nothing fundamental about it and is to be found nowhere except in the modern West. This is incredible. And what, in an altogether general way, is the sensible substance that one can touch, measure, weigh, analyze, and possibly work or shape? And why, for goodness' sake, would this not be matter?

I do not know from where Guénon gets this enumeration of the five conditions of physical existence which he calls 'corporeal': space, time, form, number, and life. I am in agreement as regards the first four, but not as regards life, because what we are concerned with here is matter or, if one prefers, physical substance. If one adds life, which is not at all a general condition, it is likewise necessary to add other secondary categories such as color and so on. The

Guénonians solemnly maintain that it is a question, not of life as vital force, but of a condition much more subtle and altogether general, which is absurd for two reasons: firstly, because it does not explain the absence—in the enumeration—of matter, and secondly, because this 'life' which is spoken of is not something that we can observe in the same way as we observe, without any difficulty, space, time, form, number, and matter. And if this mysterious thing named in fifth place is not what we call life, why give it that name?

❖

ONE MAY, with good reason, wonder at the offhand manner with which Guénon treats entire peoples. He does not hesitate to say: 'the Greeks, however mendacious they may have been.' According to him, the Japanese constitute for the East an 'anomaly' and 'do not truly belong to the yellow race'; they have virtually no right to exist seeing that modernism, hence error, suits their mentality better 'after all' than does Chinese civilization, which they made the mistake of 'copying without real assimilation.' It would be easy to refute these excesses. 'There is,' it seems, 'nothing more dissimilar than a German and a Hindu'—which, be it said in passing, is complete nonsense from the anthropological point of view; and the Germans are only capable of producing encyclopedias which, we are told, has the advantage of sparing a tedious labor 'to those who are capable of something else,' the French no doubt. 'As to the intellectuality of the Russians, it were better not to speak of it'; may one know what is the special demerit of Russian theologians, and in what way Russian philosophers of the nineteenth century are less 'intellectual' than their French *confrères*, such as Comte or Taine? The Latins, according to Guénon, are less remote from the East than the Germans—which is an error, because there are, at the very most, certain differences of accent in the common remoteness.

'For us,' writes Guénon in *East and West*, 'the modern spirit originated above all in the German and Anglo-Saxon countries; it is in these same countries, naturally, that it is most deeply rooted and will live longest. . . .' Really? What about the Renaissance? And

Cartesianism? And the Encyclopedists? And the French Revolution? Have not all these created the modern world and have they not contributed powerfully to corrupting the Germanic countries?

Speaking of the Western hatred of Islam, Guénon is of the view that 'fear contributes a good share of the motives for this hatred' and that 'this state of mind is due only to incomprehension'! That the West is of Christian substance, and that Islam rejects the Divinity of Christ and the legitimacy of the Church, seems to have escaped Guénon, who 'does not see the wood for the trees.' Then, if there is something which certainly does not contribute to motives for the hatred of Islam, it is fear; the Europeans of the nineteenth century had no reason, absolutely none, to fear the Muslim world and their politics prove it. And if, on the other hand, they had a certain fear of the 'yellow peril'—for which Guénon reproaches them—history is there to show them that they were by no means wholly mistaken!

Here is an altogether characteristic example from *East and West*:

> These 'young' Easterners, as they call themselves in order better to indicate their leanings, could never gain a real influence among them; sometimes, without their knowledge, they are made use of in order to play a role which they do not suspect, and that is all the easier because they take themselves so seriously. . . .

Everything is there: the overestimation of Eastern humanity and next the theory of puppets, typical for Guénonian 'mythology', without forgetting the little piece of perfectly gratuitous sarcasm.

In his *Introduction to the Study of the Hindu Doctrines*, Guénon speaks of the 'main divisions of the East'; one of them, the Far East, ends with China at Tongking and Annam; Japan, 'which we have left to one side in our general classification,' docs not form part of the Far East! Yet, at the time when Guénon published this book, Turkey was Kemalist; this did not suffice to cast Turkey into disgrace similar to that of Japan, nor to revise the judgement passed on the latter in proportion to the indulgence accorded Turkey. The infallible authority of Guénon had, as regards the yellow people of the East, a single source: Albert de Pouvourville who, in the end, converted to Catholicism! And that after having initiated Guénon in the name of Tong-Sang-Laut; this Taoist dignitary died, it appears, while Guénon was still at school. But to return to Turkey: 'these "young" Easterners . . . could never gain a real influence among them,' deems Guénon; and he publishes this opinion after a dozen years of Kemalist rule! However, the Japanese, for their part, have never hanged bonzes on the charge of failing to dress as Europeans!

The Guénonians will say that all this is of no importance; it is of the order of contingencies, not of principles. Now, leaving aside that this *distinguo* could lead us very far, it is, on the contrary, very important, not only because Japan constitutes an essential part of the Far East, but also because the opinions in question betoken a singular manner of observing, evaluating, and 'reasoning'—whenever the 'dogmas' of the system appear to be threatened.

Thus, the Chinese republic of *Sun-Yat-Sen* does not disturb Guénon; it is something 'tolerated as transitory,' given that China 'has always absorbed its successive conquerors.' He forgets that these conquerors were more or less barbarian people of the yellow race who, without fail, were bound to be integrated into Chinese civilization—a case similar to that of the Goths who, having reached southern Europe, were necessarily integrated into Roman civilization; and he forgets more particularly that nothing in history is comparable to the modern spirit, which alone corrupts every spiritual and traditional value. It is unbelievable that it is Guénon who forgets this; and that he forgets it because what is at issue is China classified within the category 'East'—the supposedly incorruptible East—by the Count de Pouvourville alias Matgioi, while Japan—reservoir of all Far-Eastern values—is fiercely excluded therefrom.

❖

IN A GENERAL WAY, the following conclusion is inescapable: Guénon is magisterial in his defense of the traditional East and his condemnation of the anti-traditional West, but he overestimates Eastern man as such and underestimates Western man as such. One

might also say that he demolishes with the left hand what he con-
structs with the right; this would scarcely be an exaggeration. He
addresses himself to the West but, as a matter of fact, he leaves the
West nothing except Freemasonry—a highly problematic affair—
and a 'Christian tradition' which concretely has every right to symbolism but which, abstractly and as an esoterism, merely begs the
question; this conjectural Christianity is also allowed the right to be
the 'exoteric complement' of the aforementioned Masonry! Western
intellectuality? It amounts to Aristotelian Scholasticism; Guénon
has a curiously poor regard for Neoplatonism, and he admitted to
me that he had never read Meister Eckhardt. Western sanctity? It
amounts in fact to 'mysticism', a spirituality which, so it would
appear, is 'passive', exoteric, profane, and very concerned with 'phenomena'; an opinion which proves that Guénon is ignorant of mystical theology. It is no more than an exoterism; so there is no
occasion to look in that quarter for an 'initiatic' attachment. Western esoterism? It emigrated after the destruction of the Templars;
but, happily, there remains Masonry and the Compagnonnage! We
must therefore seek to demodernize them, especially Masonry;
Christianity will then be good enough to be added to it in the
capacity of 'technically indispensable exoterism'. Question: where
does the Christian find any trace of all this in the words of Christ—
in which he places his trust because their authority is Divine, and
whose claims are consequently absolute? It is true that we are told
there must also be a Catholic initiation, but 'in such restricted circles that in point of fact they can be considered to all intents and
purposes inaccessible. . . .' The Hesychast initiation, which is
referred to in passing, is nothing but a gratuitous assumption; all
the same, if Hesychasm did possess a supra-sacramental initiation,
which is precisely what is excluded, it would not be accessible to
Catholics. The sacraments? Heaven, it seems, has withdrawn from
them their initiatic efficacy; and there it is. I shall say not only that
this privation or restriction is impossible, but also that it would be
profitless; it would confer nothing on the simple man and would
deprive the elect of everything. The miracles of the saints? Mere
'phenomena' deserving the scorn of those who concern themselves
with 'serious matters'!

Guénon sees everywhere in the West 'total ignorance'; he does not notice that it is far more a case of a refusal to accept than of ignorance pure and simple. The West is not necessarily—and totally!—ignorant of certain truths; it can even note them very well, but hardens itself against them; it closes its ears, and therein lies the drama and the crime of the West. When the Westerner is told that he is ignorant of everything, that he has no idea—not the slightest— of anything, and is then presented with a Sufi treatise, for example, he is at once bewildered, disappointed, and indignant, he who knows Plotinus, Meister Eckhardt, and Angelus Silesius, to mention only these three.

True, there are: pure metaphysics, the relationship between esoterism and exoterism, initiation, doctrinal and methodical gnosis, traditional civilizations, the modern error; but traditional values do not present themselves exactly as Guénon would have it. They are sometimes much simpler, their mystery is often relative or even more or less accidental; things are not so hidden and inaccessible; it is chiefly man that makes them so from the fact that he does not wish to hear anything about them and that he per- secutes those who understand more than he himself wishes to understand. And all this is much less total and less administrative than Guénon imagines; there are not only causal relationships of a 'horizontal' kind, there is also the unforeseen, which is 'vertical' in nature. Admittedly, there is traditionally that which is secret, but it is less arrogant and often more contingent than Guénon thinks; paradoxically, Guénon seems readily to lose sight of the fact that doctrine is always something relatively outward; he is the first to admit it, but in fact, he often appears to forget it, and this is not the least of his inconsequence.

When Guénon sees fit 'formally to state' that 'there is, to our knowledge, no one in the West who has expounded authentic Eastern ideas, other than ourself,' one is entitled to feel amazed and to concede, at the very least, extenuating circumstances to Guénon's orientalist adversaries. At the end of a chapter in his *Theosophy: History of a Pseudo-Religion*, Guénon declares that there is, in the East, nothing which even distantly resembles the idea of reincar- nation; has he then never read the *Mānava-Dharma-Shāstra*? It is extremely distressing, when one has no interest in criticizing Guénon—on the contrary, one has, a *priori*, an interest in supporting him—to have to recognize that his adversaries are better informed and sometimes even show more understanding than he; it is all the more distressing, seeing that it was not they who began the squabble. Be that as it may, what matters to us is not the prestige of a given author, but the Truth, and Guénon himself has not failed expressly to insist on this *distinguo!*

❖

According to Guénon the distinction between the 'possible' and the 'real' has no meaning, since, metaphysically, every possibility has its own reality. As though the one precluded the other! Very often, when Guénon criticizes an idea which, according to him, is 'Western' or 'philosophical', one would like to answer him: but the one does not preclude the other; the metaphysical Infinite does not preclude space from being infinite in its own way. According to him, the notion of infinitude is metaphysical by definition; by what right? What is infinite is, quite simply, that which has no end: nothing else. It is a characteristic feature with Guénon that metaphysical meanings cause him to lose sight of physical ones; it is as though one were to reject the data of planimetry by reference to three dimensional geometry while alleging, for example, that a circle is not round because it is not a sphere.

The criterion of what the word 'possible' can legitimately be taken to mean is what it means in an immediate manner; what is possible is what can either be or not be, for example a journey, or what proves its possibility by its existence, for example a vegetable species. Strictly speaking, things might not be, since necessary being belongs by right to the Divine Principle alone, but they are because Existence is relatively necessary in virtue of the radiating power of Being, and because contingency, and hence diversity, is in its turn necessary in function of the principle of particularization, or individuation, proper to Existence.

The distinction between the possible and the real appears to me to be justified when one envisages things, as one usually does, from the starting-point of a particular order of reality. For example, that a given man may undertake a given journey is possible, but—as he will not undertake it—it is not real, although, on the universal scale, this possibility as such is real in its turn. The perspective of the reality of fact and that of the reality of principle, or being, do not exclude one another any more than do the point of view of morality and that of ontological necessity; here again, the universal point of view transcends and abolishes—or, in a certain sense, absorbs—the distinction established from the human point of view.

In order to distinguish Non-Being from Being, I might say that the first is 'infinitely infinite' whereas the second is 'relatively infinite', which, while being tautological and contradictory, is nevertheless a useful turn of phrase in a necessarily elliptical language; the disparity between logic and truth means that the latter can sometimes violate the former, whereas the inverse is excluded. If we exclude Non-Being, we are entitled to ascribe infinitude to Being; but if we consider Non-Being, I would say it is Non-Being that is infinite, and that Being is only an already relative aspect thereof. But I would never say that 'when one opposes Non-Being to being . . . neither the one nor the other is infinite, since, from this point of view, they limit each other in a certain fashion'; nor would I say that 'infinity belongs only to Being and Non-Being taken together,' because that would be to introduce into the metaphysical domain ways of thinking that are excessively mathematical and fundamentally absurd.

❖

IN HIS ARTICLE 'Ascending and Descending Realization',[1] Guénon puts forward, as scriptural basis and traditional justification for his thesis, the four states of *Ātmā*, namely *Vaishvānara*, *Taijāsa*, *Prājna*, and *Turīya*—'wakefulness', 'dream', 'deep sleep', and 'unconditioned

---

1. *Initiation and Spiritual Realization* (Hillsdale: Sophia Perennis, 2004), ch. 32.

state'—these four states representing also, for man, the stages of spiritual realization; for total Deliverance implies the perfection of formal and informal manifestation, and then the realization of onto-logical and supra-ontological non-manifestation, namely Being and Non-Being.

The 'fourth state', *Turīya*, corresponds to Non-Being. On this subject Guénon says in *Man and His Becoming according to the Vedānta*, in the chapter referring to this state [chap. 15]:

> In itself then *Ātmā* is neither manifested [*vyakta*] nor unmanifested [*avyakta*], so long at least as one only regards the unmanifested as the immediate principle of the manifested [which refers to the state of *Prājna*]: but it is the principle both of the manifested and the unmanifested [although this Supreme Principle can also be said to be unmanifested in a higher sense].

The idea of the unmanifested therefore has two different meanings: there is the absolute unmanifested, *Paramātmā* or *Brahma nirguna*, and the relative unmanifested *Māyā* or *Īshvara* or *Brahma saguna*. This relative unmanifested, Being, can be called the potentially manifested with respect to the actually manifested, the world. To say that the absolute unmanifested is the principle both of the unmanifested and the relative unmanifested is, however, a tautol-ogy: since it is the principle of Being, Non-Being is implicitly the principle of Existence; it is improper to say that it is the principle both of Being and Existence, because this expression gives Existence a false independence with respect to Being and a false reality with respect to Non-Being.

Now in his article on descending manifestation Guénon says that 'beyond these three states' (*Vaishvānara, Taijāsa, Prājna*)—hence beyond the unmanifested itself—there is a fourth one which can be said to be 'neither manifested nor unmanifested, since it is the principle of both, but which also, for that reason, comprises them both.'

This last assertion, which seems to have been prompted by an untoward speculation by Coomaraswamy, makes no sense in my opinion because the words 'neither manifested nor unmanifested' do not mean 'beyond this alternative in the absolute sense'; they mean simply that the absolute unmanifested, Non-Being, is beyond the relative unmanifested, Being, and the manifested which proceeds from it; or, in other words, that it is beyond the potentially manifested as well as the actually manifested. From the point of view of the absolute manifested the distinction between the potentially manifested—or the relative and creative unmanifested—and the effective manifested or the created (hence between Being and Existence) has no reality; in relation to Non-Being, it is neither a duality nor a complementarity nor an alternative. *Paramātmā* does not have to pay the illusory price of an opposition which, even at the degree of *Īshvara*, is most problematic; for also in relation to Being, the manifested is null.

It is appropriate to envisage: first, the Absolute in itself, and second, the Absolute insofar as it deploys itself as *Māyā*, or in the mode of *Māyā*. In this second respect, 'everything is *Ātmā*; it is *Allah* as *Zāhir*, 'the outward'. In an analogous manner, things can be envisaged: firstly, in themselves in respect of their separate existence, and secondly, within Being as archetypes. Every aspect of relativity—even principial—or of manifestation is *vyakta*; and every aspect of absoluteness—even relative—or of non-manifestation is *avyakta*.

Coomaraswamy, whom Guénon cites in the article under discussion, considers that

> it is necessary to have passed beyond the manifested . . . in order to reach the unmanifested . . . but the highest goal lies yet beyond the unmanifested; the end of the way is not reached until *Ātmā* is known both as manifested and unmanifested.

And Guénon, who takes him at his word, doubtless because Coomaraswamy draws his inspiration from the *Katha Upanishad*, concludes thus:

> In order to attain this, it is therefore necessary to go 'beyond darkness', or, as certain texts express it, 'to see the other face of darkness.'

Now this 'beyond darkness' is quite clearly the intrinsic luminosity of the Self, which appears after the darkness presented by the unmanifested in comparison with the luminosity of the manifested.

Fundamentally, to pass from *Prājna* to *Turīya*—or from the relative or ontological unmanifested to the absolute or supra-ontological unmanifested—is to pass from *Māyā* to *Ātmā*; but I absolutely fail to see why this passage should necessitate returning in any way whatsoever to the manifested, for this would be incompatible with the infinitude of *Ātmā* and contrary to the transcendent reality of the Principle. Guénon foresees the objection and seeks to refute it thus: 'It cannot be said definitively that the manifested is strictly negligible, although it may appear so in relation to the unmanifested'; reading this assertion, one thinks one is dreaming, seeing that the word 'negligible' signifies nothing on the metaphysical plane, and seeing that Guénon himself has underlined on other occasions that manifestation is 'rigorously null in relation to the Principle.'

Moreover, supposing there to be 're-descent', hence return to manifestation in a superior sense, I absolutely fail to see why this return should take the form of a specific activity among men, and thus of a submersion in such and such particular human, and historical, contingencies. This activity, whether one calls it a 'mission' or something else, does not seem to me to have any connection with what might constitute a transcendent penetration of the manifested world—assuming, that is to say, that the latter represents a possibility and a necessity. And it represents a possibility in the form of the gift of major miracles, not otherwise.

The realization corresponding to *Turīya* necessarily involves a transcending of the complementarity between the manifested, *Samsāra*, and its Principle, *Īshvara*; but it is pointless to refer to this complementarity since the transcending of *Īshvara* implies *ipso facto* the transcending of *Samsāra*. This realization is the transcending of *Māyā*, and *Māyā* embraces both *Īshvara* and *Samsāra*. Now in the Self, the question of a manifestation no longer arises; there is therefore no sense in the idea of any recapitulation of the created, apart from what, in realization, in any case takes place with respect to the world around us.

❖

GUÉNON SEEMS TO HAVE a kind of allergy against anything that is properly human, whence, for example, his option for 'ritual' in preference to 'morality'. In this same chapter, on 'descending realization', he says that for the being realizing the unmanifested 'there is no longer any ego, that is to say individuality, the limitation constituting it having necessarily been abolished.' Further on he says that 'descending realization' is a 'sacrifice', but immediately adds that he does not employ this word

> in the simply 'moral' sense which is commonly given to it, this exception being only one example of that degeneration of modern language which diminishes and denatures all things, in order to bring them down to a purely human level and make them fit the conventional bounds of 'ordinary life'.

For his part, he takes 'this word in its true and original sense, including everything effective and even essentially "technical" that it implies....' We are therefore warned: the spiritually 'descending' being has no ego and, in any case, his 'sacrifice' cannot be what is 'commonly' understood by this word. But further on, the author speaks of the 'hesitations' that these beings go through at the prospect of their sacrifice and their temptation to remain in the 'night' of the unmanifested, circumstances which he considers 'can be understood without difficulty'; may I enquire why, given that those concerned no longer have any ego and that the sacrifice is not a sacrifice? It appears that it is for the reason indicated—according to Coomaraswamy—namely, that Shankara always strove visibly 'to avoid consideration of "re-descent" even when he comments on texts whose sense clearly enough involves it,' and that such an attitude 'can ... only be understood as a sort of shrinking from the prospect of the "sacrifice"....' Why this shrinking, I repeat, since the sacrifice has nothing moral about it and since, furthermore, there is no longer any ego? It is, moreover, curious to conclude, when an author fails to express some opinion, that he fails to do so because he hesitates to do so; logic like this could take us a long way!

I could add that I do not see any connection, not the slightest, between a sacrifice in the current and moral sense of the word and 'ordinary life'!

At the end of the chapter, Guénon poses the following question: 'since the states of the being are of an indefinite multiplicity, how could that prevent our accepting the possibility of every being, in one state or in another, attaining to this supreme degree of the spiritual hierarchy?'—namely to the degree of the Founders of religion. I say 'no' to this unrealistic and extravagant opinion, for reasons which I do not believe it is necessary to explain, more especially as I have treated of all these question in my article 'The Mystery of the Bodhisattva'.[1]

But nothing can exceed my amazement when I read in a note that

> it is precisely with this signification that the inverted triangle is taken as the symbol of the highest grades in Scottish Masonry; moreover, as the 30th degree in this branch of Masonry is regarded as the *nec plus ultra*, it must logically mark thereby the end of the 'ascent' so that, strictly speaking, the succeeding degrees can only refer to a 're-descent', through which the influences destined to 'vivify' it are conveyed to the whole initiatic organization. . . .

And there it is! However, Masonry is a craft initiation, if indeed it has remained one—but that is not now the question—and we have been told that it aims at the realization of the 'primordial state', which is equivalent to the goal of the 'lesser mysteries'; we are then asked to believe that in the bosom of such a brotherhood men methodically pursue the realization, not only of the 'greater mysteries', but even of the spiritual supereminence of the Prophets! And where, may it be asked in passing, do these totally unrealistic and syncretistic 'high degrees' come from, since they are so completely disproportionate in their nature to the greatness of the *Avatāras?* It would seem that Masonry gives rise to the supreme degree—if this word 'degree' still has any meaning here—of universal spirituality, and then administratively records, defines, and

---

1. *Treasures of Buddhism*, pp107–134.

labels it; has it ever been known for an *Avatāra* to allow himself to be regimented within the prefabricated hierarchy of a secret society? And why this utterly mad and unheard of extravagance of an *Avatāric* presence? In order to 'convey to the whole initiatic organization'—namely Scottish Masonry—'the influences destined to "vivify" it'!

Nevertheless, in his article 'Les hauts grades maçonniques', published in 1910 in *La Gnose*,[1] Guénon-Palingénius notes that in most of the high-grade systems 'one encounters incoherences, gaps, and redundancies,' and that 'this multiplicity of degrees is all the more useless given that one is obliged to confer them in series.' And further on he says:

> contrarily to what has often been maintained, the knight Ramsey was not the inventor of the high grades, and ... if he is responsible for them, it is only indirectly, because those who conceived the Scottish system took their inspiration from an address delivered by him in 1737, in which he linked Masonry both with the Mysteries of antiquity and, more immediately, with the religious and military orders of the Middle Ages.

A little later, the author says of the high grades: 'we consider that they have an incontestable practical utility but on condition—unfortunately too seldom realized, especially today—that they really fulfill the purpose for which they were created.' By the end of the article, the author thinks he

> has said enough about this to give an indication of what the high Masonic grades could be if, instead of wishing to abolish them purely and simply, one were to make of them true initiatic centers for the transmission of esoteric science. ...

But all this has no connection, absolutely none, with the transcending of *Māyā* at the degree of the *Bodhisattvas* and *Avatāras*! Why then, for goodness' sake, was it necessary to include in the article on 'descending realization' the impossible note about Scottish Masonry?

1. See *Studies in Freemasonry and the Compagnonnage*, Annex 6. ED.

Grosso modo, a 'descending realization' could have the following meaning: there is a spirituality which isolates itself from the world of phenomena and encloses itself, if one may so express it, in the blessed obscurity of inward contemplation; but there is another spirituality, proceeding from the first, for which the world reveals itself as an aspect of the Principle; this is 'to see God everywhere', so that in practice there is no longer any opposition between 'outward' and 'inward'. Krishna, in loving the *Gopīs*, is *Purusha* loving the possibilities of *Prakriti;* and in waging holy war, the *Avatāra* is *Shiva* who overcomes *Tamas* or *Avidya*, or he is *Ātmā* who dissolves in *Māyā*. At a given moment the saint can leave his cave and mingle with the world, not because his spiritual degree obliges him to do so, but because the reason for his isolation no longer exists; whether God then imposes on the saint a mission that he hesitates to accept is an altogether different question, and one which is unrelated to the nature of his spiritual state—although this nature is obviously a *conditio sine qua non* of the Divine mandate. It is by 'seeing God everywhere' that the saint possesses such a degree—and not by fulfilling a mission that presupposes this degree. In Sufism, this is the degree of *Jalwa* that follows *Khalwa*—the 'radiation' that follows the 'retreat'.

❖

Even in Guénon's best books one is confronted with assertions which, to say the least, are problematic, such as the following from chapter two of *Man and His Becoming according to the Vedānta*:

human individuality is both much more and much less than Westerners usually believe: much more, because they know scarcely anything except the corporeal modality, which represents only a minute portion of its possibility; much less, because this individuality, far from really constituting the being, is only one state of that being among an indefinite number of other states, the sum of which is still nothing in relation to the personality, which alone is the true being.

Really? Do Christians know only the corporeal modality of the individuality? And do not unbelievers have the notion of psychology? Are not Christians aware that the human individual, like the entire world, is but nothing before God? And what does he mean by 'the total being'? If it is the totality of all cosmic subjectivities, from vegetables to angels, who has ever dreamt of deducing the human individual's insignificance from this multitude of creatures, taking as starting point the notion of the segmentation of the Universal Subject? For the perception of that insignificance does not require this detour, and it is extraordinary, to say the least, to see in man not a being, but a 'state of the total being'; as though the one excluded the other, and as though one could ascribe to the human individual an indefinite number of modalities or possibilities by referring to the cosmic subjectivities, with which he is obviously linked by virtue of the homogeneity of the Universe.

Such at least is the first reaction to the passage quoted; but on reading other passages, for example in *The Multiple States of the Being*, especially at the beginning of chapter two, which shows that these states can be classified as 'pre-human' or 'post-human', we eventually realize that what is in question is transmigration. Thus, after a maze of dizzying abstractions, we learn that 'the total being' is the subject envisaged in relation to the total cycle of its lives, and that it is precisely these lives that constitute the 'states of the being'; and so at least we understand what the author is talking about! It is true that—according to Guénon—concrete expressions are too human and heavy with prejudice, so that it is consequently advisable to be as abstract as possible, at any rate when speaking to Westerners. For Easterners it is a different matter: Their concrete language belongs to symbolism, which is infinitely superior to the abstractions of philosophy; they can therefore allow themselves the luxury of speaking in terms of reincarnation without incurring any blame; the demerit of taking them literally belongs to Westerners!

By presenting Guénon's views and their logical consequences in this way, I am obviously not referring either to the symbolism or to the abstraction—if the latter does not pointlessly cut itself off from the key image; I refer solely to the contradiction of a dialectic which is inordinately abstract—based on the one hand on the axiom of the primacy of the pure symbol, and on the other on contempt for the abstract or non-symbolic character of the 'profane' language of philosophers; and furthermore I regret in this instance the silence regarding the traditional landmarks. Certainly one finds geometrical symbolism in Guénon's works, but it stops short half-way between image and abstraction, and it is not this that East-erners use *a priori* when they speak of transmigration.

As regards the doctrine of the 'multiple states', I would say that it is important to distinguish between the more or less descriptive viewpoint of cosmology and the properly metaphysical perspective, which envisages things not so much according to their horizontal relationships but more according to their intrinsic or essential meanings. One may thus establish the following *distinguo*:

First: from the cosmological point of view, it is the total samsāric cycle, and by extension the totality of all samsāric cycles, that constitutes what Guénon calls 'the total being' or 'true being'. This is the 'horizontal' perspective, which is represented geometrically by concentric circles.

Second: from the metaphysical point of view—and this is the 'vertical' perspective, represented geometrically by converging rays—the concrete being (one defined by a particular form) is 'the true being', and this is so precisely to the extent that the form is 'central'—as it is for the human being—and to the extent that the being thereby attaches itself more or less consciously to the Absolute. For an ant, the samsāric cycle takes precedence before the accidental state of being an insect; but for man, on the contrary, it is the human, and hence theomorphic, personality—'made in the image of God'—that takes precedence before the preparatory samsāric cycle, more especially as the human condition by definition embraces all peripheral states. The human person of the *Avatāra* cannot be just any 'state' of being that is anonymous, protean, and, so to speak, abstract because without form or face.

To speak of the 'state' of a being is to speak, for example, of wakefulness or sleep, of youth or old age, of health or sickness, of pleasure or suffering, or of faith or unbelief, in respect of one and the same identifiable subject. When the subject is not identifiable, which happens when there is discontinuity from one state to another—in other words when each 'state', instead of adding itself to the being, creates a new being—the question arises as to whether one is still justified in calling this new and concrete being a 'state', or whether it is not rather the 'vertical' determination, the integrating and personifying ray of the Self, which conditions and characterizes the true being. Conclusion: the answer to the question of knowing whether it is the samsāric cycle or, on the contrary, the central person, who is 'the true being', depends on the degree of theomorphism of the being or 'state' envisaged.

There is no reason to attribute more reality to the concentric circle than to the centripetal ray; the circle determines the degree of existence, but the ray, in its turn, determines the personality, and hence participation in the Self.

Existence is made up of containers, contents, and modalities. Containers: these are the planes whose hierarchy of levels is brought about by the reverberation of the Self; they involve the segmentation of the reflected Image, and this by reason of their degree of relativity or remoteness. Contents: these are the reflected images just mentioned, diversified precisely by the planes of existence. Modalities: these are the effects of the existential diversification affecting the images themselves; in other words, the contents or images imply cycles of modalities by reason of the image's relativity or remoteness from the Self. Each reflection of the Self, to the extent that it is relative, comprises cycles; each 'form' is limited by definition, and this limit affects not only its nature—which is specific, particular, and exclusive—it also affects its presence in the world, which has a beginning and an end, and which we call a 'life'. 'Space' and 'time' are not merely earthly hazards, they are the earthly reflections of universal principles which intervene—to one degree or another—wherever there is existence, and hence infra-principial relativity, cosmic *Māyā*; the modes or systems vary, but the principles are the same.

There are 'circles' of existence, and 'rays' of principial determination: to the concentric circles correspond the *Bodhisattvas* and the point of view 'Divine Presence'; to the rays (convergent or centripetal) correspond the *Buddhas* and the point of view 'spiritual function'. But from a certain point of view they are identical, and this identity can be represented by a spiral, or by a cross inscribed in a circle, the first figure being dynamic, and the second static.

Guénon gives the impression that transmigration is a journey through equivalent 'states', none of which is 'privileged', and where the chances of attaining the supreme goal, or of not attaining it, are always the same; he never speaks of hell and he seems strangely to lose sight of the fact that 'human birth is hard to obtain'—that the human condition is therefore actually privileged, whatever may be our metaphysician's aversion to everything human. An Eastern text compares the chance of entering the human state to the chance that a turtle has of putting its head through a ring of wood floating somewhere on the ocean; this amounts to saying that the relation between the fragmentary or passive states, and a total or active state, is that between the periphery and the center—which is no small thing, and which explains the imperative insistence of religions and spiritual methods on putting our human condition to good use.

> Far from being an absolute and complete unity in himself, as most Western philosophers—at any rate modern ones without exception—would hold, the individual constitutes only a relative and fragmentary unity. He is not a closed and self-sufficient whole . . . and the notion of 'individual substance', understood in this sense . . . has no truly metaphysical import: basically, it is nothing else than the logical notion of 'subject'. . . . The individual, even when envisaged in the full extension of which he is capable, is not a total being, but only a particular state of manifestation of a being, a state . . . occupying a certain place in the indefinite series of states of the total being.

So writes Guénon, in chapter one of *The Symbolism of the Cross*. To this I reply: the fact that the individual has about him something relative and fragmentary, on account of his ontological remoteness from the Principle, in no way precludes his representing a real unity in his own order, and this is by virtue of the 'relatively absolute' which has to be realized at every level of existence; it is therefore perfectly legitimate to speak of an 'individual substance', and I do not in any way see by what right one can reduce the concrete reality of the human individual to the simple logical notion of subject. The individual is well and truly—and by definition—a total being within the framework of his existential relativity, and experience

proves this superabundantly: the 'ego' of the saint empties itself of
the world and is filled with God; it goes to Paradise and is extin-
guished—at various degrees or according to various modes—in the
Divine Self; the saint in Heaven may well have a unitive and Divine
dimension, but his celestial body, guarantee of his identity, is always
there, and when the saint miraculously manifests himself on earth,
as the Holy Virgin does, what is manifested is always the same 'ego',
the same subjectivity, the same continuity, the same immortal and
irreplaceable kernel 'made in the image of God'.

In *The Multiple States of the Being*, chapter four, Guénon once
again remarks, not without a preliminary blow at the expense of
'Western and profane psychology', that

> the alleged unity of the 'ego'... is a fragmentary unity since it
> relates only to a part of the being, namely, to one of its states
> taken arbitrarily, and in isolation, from among an indefinite
> number of others (and even this state is usually very far from
> being envisaged in its integrality); but this unity, even considered
> in relation only to this special state, is still as relative as possible
> because the latter is itself composed of an indefinite number of
> diverse modifications [etc., etc.].

One sees plainly what the author has in mind: the 'ego' changes with
its contents—the old man is a different 'ego' from the child—but this
fact nevertheless does not abolish either the continuity between the
child and the old man, or the unity of the ego upon which this
continuity depends; and the unity of the subject is all the more
pronounced when the intellectual and moral level is elevated, in
other words when the individual realizes the human norms in
sufficient plenitude. For Guénon, only the Self possesses unity, and
it follows for him that the 'ego' is diverse and fluctuating; he forgets
that the human 'ego' is both one and stable through participation in
the Self which is the raison d'être of humanity; in other words, the
Self seeks, not only to be Itself, but also to manifest Itself within
relativity by conferring upon the reflected image a certain participation in its own absoluteness. And this is enough, not assuredly to
claim that manifestation is equal to the Principle, but to recognize

that the homogeneity of the 'ego' has about it something 'relatively absolute', and that its unity is therefore genuine and represents in its own way a total being; otherwise it could be neither the point of departure for, nor the support of, deification.

What distinguishes one ego from another is intelligence on the one hand and virtue on the other or, on the contrary, their absence; and these qualities or privations are independent of sensorial impressions and emotions: they are fundamental characteristics that determine the worth of the individual and confer upon him a movement which is either ascending or descending. Man, when fully conformable to his human vocation, is not only a series of states of consciousness but above all a spiritual nature, and hence a realization of love of God; and God does not address himself to insignificant modalities, but to whole persons.

Guénon, with his mathematician's aversion to everything concrete and human, strangely—and tragically—loses sight of the intrinsic quality of subjectivity; whence his eagerness to dissolve the human person who, for him, is 'metaphysically' odious, in a system of numberless abstractions; what remains is an abstract 'modality' lacking any content, or any reference to the Absolute. Now for God, man is a 'valid interlocutor', which excludes his being only a fragmentary state without real stability. Man is the 'vicar of God on earth', which is no small thing, and which is not just anything.

❖

AT THE BEGINNING of his article 'Christianity and Initiation',[1] Guénon informs us that he has

> never felt any inclination specially to treat this subject, for various reasons, the first of which is the almost impenetrable obscurity surrounding everything having to do with the origins and early days of Christianity; this obscurity is so great that it

---

1. *Insights into Christian Esoterism*, (Hillsdale: Sophia Perennis, 2004), chap. 2.

appears, on careful reflection, that it cannot be merely accidental but, rather, must have been expressly intended.

Question: since this obscurity, supposing it exists, does not prevent the author from having an altogether clear and peremptory opinion on the sacraments, why does he not have 'any inclination . . . to treat this subject,' and how is such a statement compatible—having regard to the proportions of things—with the majesty of the subject and the crucial importance of the opinion in question? For it is not 'on the margin' or 'in passing' that one lays down the law on matters that are sacred and spiritually vital.

As for the surprising opinion that the origins of Christianity are 'surrounded by an almost impenetrable obscurity,' we see no reason to accept it, and more than one reason not to accept it. We are, in fact, being asked to make an act of faith concerning a hypothesis, for if this assertion is a certainty, where are the proofs? The history of early Christianity is clear to the extent that any historical past can be; one can only suspect otherwise on the basis of a question-begging assumption. If Islam is particularly explicit with regard to its history, this is because of its perspective, which requires that the least of the acts of the Prophet be prototypes for those of the faithful: acts which will be for them supports of faith, and of the virtues demanded by it.

Naturally, nothing at the origin of a religion can be 'merely accidental'; that is perfectly clear. But what is one to think of Apostles and Fathers who would intentionally obscure the historical trails leading to the incarnate Word? Their morals were not those of a Rosicrucian or a Taoist secret society.

The absence of a social legislation does not represent a 'lacuna' for Christianity, any more than it does for Buddhism, because the integration of a pre-existing Law is precisely a possibility in cases of this kind; it is quite false to think *a priori* that every religion should have an identical exo-esoteric structure, more especially as this would be contrary to the diversity of types called for by All-Possibility.

To affirm, with the Muslims, that the early Church was a *ṭarīqa*, and hence an esoteric Order, does not in any way amount to saying that it was 'a closed or reserved organization, which did not admit everyone without distinction, but only those who possessed the necessary qualifications for receiving initiation'; for this esoterism was 'bhaktic', not 'jñānic', in nature, and if *bhakti* has an aspect of esoterism vis-à-vis *karma*—to which the Mosaic law corresponds— it has, vis-à-vis *jñāna*, an aspect of exoterism, and it is *jñāna*, or gnosis, which alone constitutes esoterism in the absolute sense. This is demonstrated, moreover, in India by the difference between monist Vishnuism and advaitic Shivaism: Vishnuism, while being initiatic after its own fashion, has nonetheless the character of a religious exoterism, at any rate in its most general aspects, whereas Shivaite Advaitism is a way reserved for an intellectual elite of brahmanic origin. When Clement of Alexandria and other Christians speak of 'secrets', they are referring to gnosis, not to Christianity in general, which, being 'bhaktic' in nature, was perfectly suited from its beginning to constitute a religion.

In 'Christianity and Initiation', we meet with the following passage which seeks to rebut our idea that the sacraments are initiatic since they were such at the beginning: 'There is in this a misunderstanding which appears to us quite evident: initiation, as we have explained many times, does indeed confer on those who receive it a character that is acquired once and for all and that is truly indelible; but the notion of the initiatic character's permanence is applicable to human beings possessing it and not to rites, or the action of the spiritual influence for which these rites are destined to serve as vehicle; it is completely unjustified to seek to transport it from one of these two cases to the other, which in fact would amount to attributing to it a completely different meaning, and we are certain that we ourself never said anything that could give rise to such a confusion.' We must own that this passage is one of the most bizarre that we have ever had occasion to behold, for it refers, with extraordinary ingenuity and a strange lack of realism, to a 'confusion' which has never entered the mind of any man; and this 'confusion', which in fact is non-existent and which is almost unimaginable as regards any normal association of ideas, is even presented as if it were the essence of the error to be rebutted! Just as extraordinary is the following passage which introduces the central thesis of the Guénonian doctrine on Christianity:

what is there to stop the same influence, or an influence of the same nature, from acting according to different modalities and in different domains, and further, as this influence is in itself of a transcendent order, must its efforts also belong to that order in every case? We do not at all see why this should be so, and we are even certain of the contrary: nor do we understand why it would be inadmissible to say that the influence that operates through the medium of the Christian sacraments, having originally acted in the initiatic order, should subsequently, in other circumstances and for reasons dependent upon these, have lowered its action to the simply religious and exoteric domain; that this occurred in such a way that its effects have ever since been limited to certain possibilities of an exclusively individual order, whose scope does not extend beyond salvation; and that it meanwhile conserved, as regards outward appearances, the same ritual supports, because these were instituted by Christ and because, without them, there would no longer even have been a truly Christian tradition.

Why this would be inadmissible, we, for our part, see without the slightest difficulty: first, for a reason of principle, which is to say that Heaven never gives less than it promises and that, in instituting the sacraments, it knew what it wished; second, for a reason of fact, which is that it is in practice impossible to modify the nature, once established, of essential traditional elements; if, quite obviously, this could not have happened during the lifetime of the Apostles, no more could it have happened later when the cycle of Revelation was closed. Christ, in instituting the Eucharist, knew what he was doing; he was not speaking for a restricted brotherhood, but for a world religion; he sent his disciples 'to preach to all nations' and spoke of his return at the end of the world. It suffices to recall the Gospel, or to read it if one has never read it, in order to recognize the obvious truth that the Church of Christ was neither a 'closed organization' (a characteristic which, as we said earlier, is in no way necessary for the relative esoterism constituted by *bhakti*) nor anything other than a religion; the originality of Christianity, in the Semitic world, lies precisely in this combination of *bhakti* and the function of *religio*.

Another reason for not accepting the change of level in the sacraments is the following: if this change were a possibility there would no longer be, in many cases, any rigorous guarantee of the stability and full efficacy of rites, which would be tantamount to chaos; and who then would determine the qualification of the human populations concerned? In some Muslim countries, there are entire populations that attach themselves to a given *ṭarīqa*, in a manner that is purely religious and not at all esoteric; the confusion between the two planes is complete, yet there is no question, either in the minds of those concerned or as regards their possibilities, of transcending the individual, and hence exoteric, domain; in these circumstances, and supposing that the effect of rites may undergo change, what would prove that the rite of affiliation has retained an initiatic character, and what reason would there be for it to possess it still? We do not see, in any case, why the Christians of the first centuries, or those of the Middle Ages, should in general have exhibited fewer real initiatic qualifications than certain Arab, Berber, or Black populations of the twentieth century. The same applies even more to Freemasons: given that they are not merely exoterist, but even irreligious, why would there not be sufficient reason for Heaven to 'lower its action', and what would prove that it did not do so as soon as a Masonry was created which was profane, 'speculative', and finally anti-clerical and anti-religious? One would indeed like to know what the principles and criteria of Heaven would be in such a case, or with what right those who accept this idea of a 'lowering' can affirm that Masonic rites are still valid. Finally, we see absolutely no reason for this 'lowering', in a case like that of Christianity, because the Spirit can in any event proportion its activity according to the capacity of the human receptacle; is God so poor that he would need to ration his graces after having granted them? Why should not one and the same rite be able to confer individual help to one, and supra-individual help to another? For he who can do the greater can do the lesser.

It is true that we are offered consolation by being told that 'lowered' or exoterized Christianity contains an esoterism; unfortunately we are informed in the same breath that this esoterism or these 'initiatic organizations ceased to exist' or 'withdrew into Asia,' or again, that what now remains of them is to be found

> in such restricted circles that, in fact, they can be considered as being to all intents and purposes inaccessible, or else ... in branches of Christianity other than the Latin Church.

In these circumstances, what reproach can be leveled against those who deem that, from the esoteric point of view which alone matters here, the 'lowering' in question—were it possible—would have been a defrauding of Western Christendom?

Moreover, if it is so plausible that a spiritual influence can lower its own level according to circumstances, why not accept at the same time that the initiation received by an individual might likewise do so in certain cases? And if there is no reason for initiation to withdraw itself from an unworthy individual, seeing that it is anyhow inoperative, why should the same not apply, and *a fortiori*, to collectivities, in which there are always exceptional individuals? If the permanence of Masonic rites, for example, constitutes the guarantee of their efficacy, it must be the same for Christian rites; if, on the other hand, this permanence of ritual form proves nothing and guarantees nothing, all becomes uncertain, and it is even useless to speak of tradition and traditional attachment.

When Guénon remarks concerning the 'lowering' of divine action in the sacraments—lowering of level that is to say, for the word 'lowering' by itself gives rise to confusion—that 'this must have been a case of an adaption which, despite the regrettable consequences that it inevitably had in certain respects, was fully justified and even necessitated by circumstances of time and place'—when Guénon makes this remark, or analogous remarks, the following objection—or obvious truth—always imposes itself: a Founder of religion knows what he wants and what he does!

We previously cited *in extenso* the passage about the 'misunderstanding' that is supposed to consist in attributing the permanence of the initiatic quality in the initiated man to the initiatic rite itself, and we did not omit to point out the extraordinary character of this demonstration; of precisely the same order is the following passage:

It is indeed obvious that the nature of early Christianity, insofar as this was essentially esoteric and initiatic, had to remain entirely unknown to those who were now admitted into a Christianity which had become exoteric; consequently, every-thing which might have revealed, or merely aroused suspicion as to what Christianity had really been at first, had to be hidden from them by an impenetrable veil. Of course, we do not need to inquire into the means whereby such an outcome could have been achieved; this would be a matter for historians, if indeed it should ever occur to them to pose this question. . . .

Even supposing that the 'lowering of level' could have taken place, we do not see why the original esoterism—in any event inaccessible to the majority of men—would have had to remain 'entirely unknown' and hidden by a tissue of equivocations; and may one know upon whom is incumbent this labor of which the author himself washes his hands with an astonishing 'of course', and with a no less astonishing gibe at the expense of the undoubtedly dumbfounded historians? And how was such a thing realizable, having regard to the rapid dispersion of the early Church? Saint Thomas, in India— or his successors—were they informed of developments? And how was it possible to guarantee the discretion of all the Christian hostlers and gladiators? We can well understand that, in these circumstances, one might 'not need to enquire into the means whereby such an outcome could have been achieved'!

Next comes the statement:

In reality, these teachings [of Christ], in their 'literalness', were neither affected nor modified by this in any way, and the continued existence of the text of the Gospels and other New Testament writings, which obviously date back to the earliest period of Christianity, constitutes a sufficient proof thereof. What has changed is solely their comprehension or, if one prefers, the perspective according to which they are envisaged and the meaning given to them in consequence; moreover, there is no reason to think that there might be anything false or illegitimate in this. . . .

No one will persuade us that Christ's disciples, Saint Mary Magdalene for example, or the majority of Saint Paul's converts, did not understand the teaching of Christ in a literal manner, as did also later Christians during nearly two millennia; we do not mean that the early Christians did not, in many cases, have a most profound knowledge—it obviously must be so at the origin of a religion—but simply that the general and millennial perspective of Christianity constitutes nothing 'new', from some given point in time, in relation to the perspective of the early Christians. 'But', continues the author,

> there are some precepts, concerning especially those who follow an initiatic way, and consequently applicable within a restricted and as it were qualitatively homogenous milieu, which in practice become unworkable if one tries to extend their application to the whole of human society; this is what people acknowledge quite explicitly by regarding them purely as 'counsels of perfection', without any obligatory character being attached to them; this amounts to saying that each man is bound to follow the way of the Gospels only to the extent ... permitted him by the contingent circumstances in which he finds himself placed, and this indeed is all that can reasonably be required of those who do not aim to go beyond ordinary exoteric practice. This exoteric practice could be defined as a necessary and sufficient minimum for assuring 'salvation', for this is the sole purpose for which it is actually intended.

If this be the case, and since according to the author official Christianity is wholly exoteric, why are there Catholics who follow the 'counsels of perfection', and what is the use of monasteries if, in order to 'assure salvation', it suffices to practice the necessary minimum practiced by worldly people? Why have all the saints insisted on more, and why did the Curé d'Ars transform his village into a sort of extramural monastery? To reduce the achieving of the soul's salvation to a question of a 'necessary minimum' is truly to simplify things to excess; it is at all events to leave out of account both man, as he concretely is, and the living God; it is all but preaching Pharisaism.

❖

FOR GUÉNON, the proof that baptism is no longer an initiatic rite is furnished by the fact that it is conferred upon anyone and 'in public', whereas in the early days of Christianity it called for 'strict precautions' and a 'long preparation'; to this we reply that the situation in the Jewish and pagan world was necessarily quite different from that within the framework of an already Christian world, and also, that the situation in a not very numerous community is different from that in a society comprising millions of members; simplification is an expedient which does not affect the essence of things. Besides, adults who become Catholics in our own day are still submitted to a fairly long preparation; only the newborn are baptized immediately. As regards urgent baptism administered by an ordinary person, possibly even by someone unbaptized, it belongs to an order analogous to that of baptism of blood, which also fails formally to satisfy the conditions of the rite; in these cases one throws oneself—precisely in the name of urgency—upon the mercy of God, and that is a domain which eludes human speculation.

In order to know whether baptism, original or not, is an initiatic rite, it suffices to know what it is deemed to confer: now a rite which removes the effect of the 'fall' and confers the virtuality of the primordial state, is thereby an initiation; to realize this virtuality is a spiritual victory which goes far beyond this 'minimum' that Guénon identifies with exoterism. The Catholic saints have nothing for which to envy the *bhaktas* of India, leaving aside, on both sides, personal differences and spiritual degrees.

After speaking of 'strict precautions', Guénon continues:

> What takes place nowadays is, in a sense, just the opposite, and it seems that everything possible has been done to facilitate in the extreme the receiving of this sacrament.

But the same is true of certain Eastern initiations not to mention Masonry. It is certainly normal for an initiatic rite to be conferred, not 'in public', but in the presence of initiates alone; but since everyone in Christian countries is baptized, the question of the 'public' does not even arise. 'If there were still a virtual initiation,' continues Guénon,

> as some have envisaged in objections which they have made to us, and if, in consequence, those who have received the Christian sacraments, or even baptism alone, had thereafter no need to seek any other initiation of whatever form, how could one explain the existence of specifically Christian initiatic organizations—such as there unquestionably were during the whole of the Middle Ages—and what in that case could have been their raison d'être, having regard to the fact that their particular rite would have represented as it were a pointless repetition of the ordinary rites of Christianity?'

As for the cumulation between sacramental initiation and the chivalric and craft initiations, we contend that there are initiations whose nature is determined by a particular vocation which constitutes the operative vehicle of the spiritual life; the chivalric initiation no more needlessly repeats the sacraments than the chivalric way needlessly repeats the Christian way. Having said that, we do not at all believe that the rites of chivalry are superior or even equal to the sacraments; and if it be allowed that certain rites of medieval Masonry might amount to an unnecessary repetition of certain Christian rites—which may be doubted in view of Masonry's purely artisanal character—the explanation lies in the pre-Christian origin of this initiation. Attachment to Hermeticism—likewise of pre-Christian origin—is explained, not by a deficiency in the Christly initiation, but by a vocational affinity for alchemy; this motivation appears to us to be entirely adequate.

'It was precisely when these initiations ceased to exist . . . that mysticism properly so-called came into being.' It may be asked what 'mysticism' is, given that Guénon attributes to this way an entirely passive and extra-initiatic character. The majority of Christian saints are what Hindus call *bhaktas*; we see no reason to envisage, as regards later Christianity, anything other than a *bhakti* of various degrees, and what distinguishes Hesychasm from Catholic spirituality is method; or, to be more exact, modern Catholicism can be reproached for lacking method, but not for lacking the basic means.

'Moreover, it is clearly understood,' continues Guénon, 'that the observance of exoteric rites is fully sufficient for attaining salvation; this is already a great deal, assuredly.' We have already replied to an opinion of this kind, which betrays a singular want of concern for the concretely and profoundly human. 'But, under these circumstances, what is to be done by those for whom, according to the expression of certain *mutaṣawwufīn*, "Paradise is still but a prison"?' It is with this phrase that the article is brought to a close. We venture to think that those of Guénon's readers who fear the 'Paradise-prison' will not be very numerous; some of them may adopt this attitude through a mixture of pedantry, pretension, and lack of imagination—characteristics which, unfortunately, one encounters only too often among contemporary aspirants to esoterism. The words in question are essentially the expression of an experience on the part of men who have penetrated the veil of *Māyā*; presented as a postulate or a program, it has about it something that is singularly disproportionate, unreal, and ill-sounding. That Paradise can be a 'prison' means: the world of phenomena, whatever it may be, is perceived as a limitation, or a system of limitations, by him who has tasted the Essence; it does not mean: Paradise is not good enough, *a priori*, for this man or that man; *quod absit*.

❖

ONE OF THE WEAKEST POINTS in the Guénonian writings is, without question, the underestimation of Western man—not of the modern world, for in this respect Guénon is a thousand times right—and correlatively the overestimation of Eastern man and the present state of the traditional civilizations. Now in order to judge of these things it is necessary above all to know what man is; it is not enough to know principles, any more than it is enough to have the notion of the 'Supreme Principle', in order to know what may or may not be done by the living God. The sense of the metaphysical imperiously demands the sense of the human, just as Truth, in so far as it is exalted, is necessarily situated in a climate of sanctity; for beauty is 'the splendor of the true'.

CONCLUSION

IT IS OBVIOUS that criticisms such as those made in the preceding pages are capable of giving rise to objections. It therefore seems appropriate to stress once more—for we are aware of the thankless-ness of our undertaking—that our criticisms are in no wise leveled at what constitutes the irreplaceable value of the Guénonian writ-ings, but uniquely at whatever, in these writings, runs the risk of prejudicing the essential.

It is essential to understand the following: at the time that Gué-non first manifested his mission, he was alone; he faced alone a world that was against him and that would and could not accept him, a world, in short, that was fundamentally hostile to him. This terrible solitude, reinforced by certain traits of character, gravely traumatized him, to the point that he saw enemies even where there were none, and hostile intentions even in benevolent attitudes; we mention these things, not in order to express any pointless blame, but simply to account for a situation which was not without its consequences, and for which, we repeat, Guénon was not entirely responsible. He had heroically crossed a bridge, and he was the first to do so; after him, others crossed this bridge; the way had been opened.

A point that we must mention in spite of its obviousness is the following: when we consider ourselves obliged to criticize certain aspects of Guénon's writings—and we do not have the choice to do otherwise—we are always aware of the perfect probity of the author: of the total absence in his character of any kind of ambition or duplicity; he was the most disinterested man that one could imagine, but he perhaps relied too much on his intelligence alone. Be that as it may, what counts above all and what has priority before all else, are obviously the constituent—and essential—elements of the Guénonian message. We refer to its contents, which, given their importance and their loftiness, cause it in fact to be a message. First of all there is the idea of tradition, and thus of traditional ortho-doxy; this is the postulate that cuts short the purely cerebral argu-mentations of all profane ideologies, however subtle or brilliant.

Then there are, and even above all, the crucial ideas of 'intellectual intuition', of 'pure metaphysics' (and thus also of pure intellectuality), that is, of esoterism and of universality, without forgetting all the questions relating to symbolism, or those touching on the mystery of spiritual realization. All of this, in Guénon's writings, entails—and determines the nature of—a masterly and courageous rejection of the modern deviation.

For us, the works of Guénon are not so much an attempt to create an 'intellectual elite', such as was envisaged — on an incontestably problematical basis—in his book *East and West,* as the radiance of pure principles: the presentation, both precise and profound, of crucial ideas, and thus of indispensable truths. And for these keys, we owe Guénon an unfailing gratitude.

FRITHJOF SCHUON
AND RENÉ GUÉNON[†]

BY PAUL SÉRANT

IN THE PREFACE to his first published work, *The Transcendent Unity of Religions*, Frithjof Schuon declared that a reading of René Guénon's works would make his own work easier to understand, just as, conversely, a reading of his work would make Guénon's easier to understand. In fact, in *The Transcendent Unity of Religions*, just as in *The Eye of the Heart*, which is as if a continuation of it, Schuon's thought seems quite close to Guénon's thought, which has 'the great merit, besides that of pure intellectuality, of either directly expounding or frequently referring to the traditional doctrines, which alone count in our eyes and which alone open up unlimited spiritual horizons.'[1] However, the tribute paid by Schuon to the great metaphysician after his death is not from a blind admirer. 'Guénon's role,' he says notably, 'was to set forth principles rather than to show their application; it was in the expression of principles that his intellectual genius was exercised with an incontestable mastery; but, for us to accept without reservation all examples and deductions proposed by the author in the course of his numerous writings, that seems a matter of opinion, and even faith, insofar as a knowledge of the facts depends on contingencies that should play no role in principial knowledge.'[2] And the last work of Frithjof Schuon, *Spiritual Perspectives and Human Facts*,[3] enables us to

---

[†] From *La Parisienne, Revue Littéraire Mensuelle*, March 1954, pp334–340.

1. *The Transcendent Unity of Religions* (London: Faber and Faber Ltd, 1953), p13.

2. *Études Traditionnelles*, special issue dedicated to René Guénon (1951), p259.

3. This article was published in 1954, and the many books Schuon published between then and his death in 1998 further substantiate Serant's remark.

understand why the author cannot accept all of Guénon's deductions (even though he does not mention him).

As we know, for Guénon, while the East has a natural aptitude for metaphysics, the West generally gains access to it only through religion, that is to say, according to him, in an incomplete and imperfect manner:

> Whereas the metaphysical point of view is purely intellectual, the religious point of view implies as a fundamental characteristic the presence of a sentimental element affecting the doctrine itself, which does not allow of its preserving an attitude of entirely disinterested speculation; this is indeed what occurs in theology, though to a degree that is more or less strongly marked according to the particular branch under consideration. This emotional element nowhere plays a bigger part than in the 'mystical' form of religious thought; and let us take this opportunity of declaring that, contrary to a far too prevalent opinion, mysticism, from the very fact that it is inconceivable apart from the religious point of view, is quite unknown in the East.[1]

This is why Guénon finds it unacceptable to speak of 'Eastern religions'; Hinduism and Taoism are essentially metaphysical and not religious. Apart from Judaism and Christianity, the term 'religion' is only appropriate for Islam, or more especially for Islam's 'social and exterior' aspect, for Islam's 'interior' aspect, Sufism, is esoteric and therefore metaphysical and not religious.

Although like Guénon he recognizes that sentimentality can be an obstacle to intellectuality, Schuon is careful to specify that intellectuality should ultimately 'engage' us in a participation of our whole being in the spiritual life. Without a moral 'qualification', a spiritual 'qualification' is practically inoperative. 'Intellectuality becomes spirituality when the whole man and not only his intelligence lives in the truth.'[2] Schuon remarks that Christ said,

---

1. *Introduction to the Study of the Hindu Doctrines* (Hillsdale: Sophia Perennis, 2004), p 81.
2. *Spiritual Perspectives and Human Facts* (Hilldsale: Sophia Perennis, 1987), p 80.

'"Blessed are the pure in heart" . . . not "Blessed are the intelligent",
which signifies that the purely contemplative quality of the intelligence is infinitely more important than its capacity to understand
such metaphysical concepts. (The 'heart', according to Schuon,
signifies the intellect and, by extension, the individual essence of
man.) Schuon likewise remarks:

> What is better in principle does not always appear so in fact; it
> may be that the virtuous act of a simple and ignorant man may
> have a secret quality that makes it more agreeable to God, not
> than metaphysics in itself, but than the soul of some particular
> metaphysician.[1]

And metaphysical certainty should be complemented by faith:

> A man may have metaphysical certainty without possessing
> 'faith', that is, without this certainty residing in his soul as an
> ever-active presence. But, if metaphysical certainty suffices on
> the doctrinal ground, it is far from being sufficient on the spiri-
> tual plane, where it must be completed and brought to life by
> faith. Faith is nothing other than the adhesion of our whole
> being to Truth, whether what we possess is a direct intuition or
> an indirect idea.[2]

The author again says that

> in faith, even if it be only belief, there is always some measure of
> certainty, and in metaphysical certainty there is always a measure
> of faith. The latter is a luminous obscurity and the former is an
> obscure light. . . .[3] It is good then never to forget that meta-
> physical certainty is not God, though it contains something of
> him. This is why Sufis accompany even their certainties with this
> formula: 'And God is more wise.'[4]

In light of these texts it seems Schuon does not draw the same

---

1. Ibid., p143.
2. Ibid., pp133–134.
3. Ibid., p135.
4. Ibid., p139.

deductions from the primacy of metaphysics as Guénon, for whom metaphysical certainty is situated infinitely above 'faith', judged to be 'sentimental' by him. It is no less interesting to confront the thought of these two metaphysicians concerning the mystical way.

According to Guénon mystical realization, while being superior to theoretical knowledge, is still quite remote from true metaphysical realization. 'In the case of mysticism,' he writes, 'the individual simply limits himself to what is presented to him and to the manner in which it is presented, having himself no say in the matter.' The mystic is thus subject to quite a variety of influences, chiefly of the sentimental order. To the 'passive' (and religious) character of the mystical way, Guénon opposes the 'active' (and metaphysical) character of the initiatic way:

In the case of initiation . . . the individual is the source of the initiative toward 'realization', pursued methodically under rigorous and unremitting control, and normally reaching beyond the very possibilities of the individual as such . . . this initiative alone does not suffice [but] it is this initiative that necessarily provides the point of departure for any 'realization'.[1]

Now Schuon considers mystical realization to be at once active and passive, and that its passive aspect is indispensable:

The passivity of the true mystic is the qualitative complement of celestial activity. When God is active the creature is passive. The participating activity of the intellect does not enter into this mode of spirituality and the activity of the will plays only an exceedingly indirect part in relation to grace. From another standpoint, however, the true mystic is active, through his ascetic discrimination, with regard to all kinds of appetites and sensations, unless these comprise an intrinsic and Divine certainty as is the case in prophecy.[2]

The total passivity spoken about by Guénon is only a matter of false mysticism: 'Only the false mystic is wholly passive. The true

1. *Perspectives on Initiation*, pp11–12.
2. *Spiritual Perspectives*, pp89–90.

mystic could not be so on the level of his will, since sanctity requires equilibrium and so force.'[1] Also, on the other hand, the mystical way is no more totally passive than the initiatic way is totally active:

> The activity of the initiate—that is of the man who possesses, in addition to initiation, a metaphysical doctrine and a correspon- ding method—cannot be taken to mean that the individual watches over and controls the Divine action, for the individual, who, precisely, has to be transcended, cannot judge what trans- cends him. That which judges is the impersonal intelligence, illuminated by the intellect, and not fluctuating and self-inter- ested thought; and that which is judged is the sum of the human repercussions of grace and not grace itself.[2]

In short, whether mysticism or initiation is involved, there is an indispensable passivity: that of man in relation to grace. For 'man always remains passive in relation to grace, exactly as reason is passive in relation to intellectual intuition.'[3] There are no spiri- tual 'techniques' which might enable man to do without divine assistance:

> Every man has need of grace, just as every man has need of faith, independently of any question of gnosis. The opposite opinion is either a question of words or else it is the worst of illusions.[4]

The basic reproach that Guénon directs against religion—and hence mysticism—was for envisioning nothing beyond the salvation of the individual, whereas the esoterism of the great metaphysical traditions has for a goal the access of the human being to Deliverance, that is 'beyond every conditioned state, whatever that may be.'

> When the mystics speak of 'union with God' [writes Guénon in one of his last studies], what they mean by this can certainly not

1. *Spiritual Perspectives*, p92.
2. Ibid., pp92–93.
3. Ibid., p93.
4. Ibid., p91.

be assimilated in any way to *Yoga*; and this remark is particularly important because some people might be tempted to say: how can a being have a higher end than union with God? All depends on the sense in which one takes the word 'union'. In reality, the mystics, like all other exoterists, are concerned with nothing more or other than salvation, although what they have in view is, if one wishes, a higher modality of salvation, for it is inconceivable that there should not also be a hierarchy among 'saved' beings. In any case, since in mystical union individuality as such subsists, it can only be a wholly exterior and relative union, and it is quite evident that the mystics have never even conceived the possibility of the Supreme Identity; they stop short at 'vision', and the entire extent of the angelic worlds still separates them from Deliverance.[1]

Here again Schuon's thought is clearly differentiated from Guénon's. Certainly the author of *Spiritual Perspectives and Human Facts*, like Guénon, adheres to the Vedantic doctrine of Supreme Identity; but he agrees that Western theology makes no mention of it: 'If theology never makes use of the direct expressions of the doctrines of identity, such as those of the Vedanta of Shankara, it is because it looks on everything in relation to man, and for it identity concerns what is inexpressible'[2] (concerning this 'inexpressible' Guénon himself says that something must be always held back, seeing that metaphysics is involved). The mystics insist above all on what separates them from God, but, for Schuon, this involves a necessary dialectic:

To say that Reality can never be attained by one who maintains the 'objective illusion' is to forget that 'union' depends, not at all on some particular terminology, but on the fusion of two distinct elements, whether we call these 'subject' and 'object' or something else; it amounts in any case to replacing the objective illusion, which is normal since it is general, by a subjective illusion, which is abnormal and therefore far more dangerous. In

1. *Initiation and Spiritual Realization*, p 48.
2. *Spiritual Perspectives*, p 169.

order to be united to something it is by no means necessary to start by pretending that one is not separate from it in any way or in any respect, or, in short, that one does not exist; one must not replace intellection by a facile and blind conviction.[1]

And, placing himself in the Vedantic perspective, Schuon specifies his thinking in these terms:

It is useless to seek to realize that 'I am *Brahma*' before understanding that 'I am not *Brahma*'; it is useless to seek to realize that '*Brahma* is my true self' before understanding that '*Brahma* is outside me'; it is useless to seek to realize that '*Brahma* is pure Consciousness' before understanding that '*Brahma* is the Almighty Creator'.

It is not possible to understand that the enunciation 'I am not *Brahma*' is false before having understood that it is true. Similarly it is not possible to understand that the enunciation '*Brahma* is outside me' is not exact before having understood that it is; and, similarly again, it is not possible to understand that the enunciation '*Brahma* is the Almighty Creator' contains an error before having understood that it expresses a truth.[2]

Therefore, here where Guénon sees a difference of nature between the mystical way and the metaphysical way, Schuon sees rather a difference of method, or even simply of formulation. And he does not hesitate to write that

the Vedantic perspective finds its equivalents in the great religions which regulate humanity, for truth is one. The formulation, however, may be dependent on dogmatic perspectives which restrict their immediate intelligibility, or which make direct expressions of them difficult of access.[3]

Schuon likewise remarks that the differences between Hindu and Christian metaphysics derive essentially from the fact that Hinduism

1. *Spiritual Perspectives*, p115.
2. Ibid., pp115–116.
3. Ibid., p101.

envisages the 'Self' (and not the human being), while in Christianity everything is envisaged in terms of the spiritual realization of man. This explains why, whereas in Hinduism knowledge seems to be self-sufficient, in Christianity, to the contrary, the accent is placed foremost on love. But these differences of method or formulation should not make us lose sight of the profound of Eastern and Western metaphysics:

> According to the Vedanta the contemplative must become absolutely 'Himself'; according to other perspectives such as that of the Semitic religions, man must become absolutely 'Other' than himself—or than the 'I'—and from the point of view of pure truth this is exactly the same thing.[1]

We are far from the hierarchy established by Guénon between the East, with its esoteric traditions, and the West, where only some initiatic societies surpass religious exoterism. Guénon clearly accepts that, at its origins, Christianity 'had both in its rites and doctrine an essentially esoteric and thus "initiatic" character,' but he adds that, since the era of Constantine and the Council of Nicea, the decomposition of the Roman world made necessary a 'descent' of Christianity into exoterism, the proof of which he notably sees in the fact that the Church has transposed truths belonging exclusively to esoterism into dogmatic terms.[2] The loss by the Church of its initiatic character would be, moreover, attested to by the existence in the Middle Ages of initiatic organizations based in Catholicism. For Schuon, Christianity is at once both exoteric and esoteric; exoteric because it presents itself as a way of love accessible to all in principle, but at the same time esoteric because its message can only be fully understood and realized by a few 'elect'. 'An exoterism,' he writes,

> can prescribe obedience to God and justice towards the neighbor; it cannot prescribe love of God and of the neighbor,

---

1. Ibid., p102.
2. *Insights into Christian Esoterism*, pp 6–11.

for these attitudes are essentially qualitative; they belong, as the Sufis would say, to the domain of 'spiritual virtue'.[1]

And the author recalls that, on the subject of Jesus, Muhyiddin ibn Arabi has commented in the following terms:

> The seal of universal sanctity above which there is no other saint is Jesus. We have met several contemplatives of the heart of Jesus.... I myself was several times united to him in my ecstasies and through his ministry I returned to God in my conversion... and he gave me the name of friend and forbade me austerity and spiritual destitution.[2]

This reference to Ibn Arabi assumes its full import once we realize that the Egyptian Shaykh 'Ilaysh al-Kabir, who initiated Guénon into Sufism (and to whom Guénon dedicated *The Symbolism of the Cross*), was considered to be one of Ibn Arabi's spiritual heirs. How could Guénon deny Christianity its esoteric character, a character acknowledged by one of the most eminent representatives of that Islamic esoterism to which he himself belonged? Why has he seen only 'sentimentality' there where Sufism sees one of the loftiest forms of spirituality? This attitude of Guénon is so much more odd if we think of how, as Schuon again points out, that 'the life of Ibn Arabi ... is interwoven with marvels, visions and miracles'[3] of an eminently 'mystical' character.

As for what concerns the initiatic societies of the Middle Ages, Schuon sees in them 'forms of esoterism that were non-Christian in origin but became christianized.'[4] The initiations conferred by these societies were limited to the cosmological realm, and it is hard to ascribe to them a 'supra-religious' import as does Guénon; they in fact are concerned with 'special vocations' which would not be in conflict with a religious point of view.

Such are, quite briefly outlined, the questions about traditional doctrine on the subject of which Schuon's thinking is clearly distinct

1. *Spiritual Perspectives*, p84.
2. Ibid., p84, n1.
3. Ibid., p88.
4. Ibid., p85.

from Guénon's. It might even be said that Schuon's positions will be gratifying to many of Guénon's readers, readers who have never been able to accept the condemnations brought by the author of *Man and His Becoming according to the Vedānta* against Western forms of spirituality. It is possible that Schuon, who above all intends to show the profound agreement between Eastern and Western traditions, goes a little too far in his resolve to 'conciliate', and thus may be inclined to attenuate some basic differences between Christianity, Islam, and Hinduism. But we ought to acknowledges that he does justice to certain aspects of Christian metaphysics on the subject of which Guénon betrays a rather surprising incomprehension.

LETTER
FROM RENÉ GUÉNON
TO FRITHJOF SCHUON

B'ismi 'Llāhi 'r-Rahmāni 'r-Rahīm;
al-hamdu li-'Llāhi wahda-Hu

Cairo, April 16, 1946

Ilā 'sh-Shaikhi 'l-fādili wa '-akhi 'l-'azīzi
Sayyidī 'Īsā Nūr ad-Dīn Ahmad.
As-salāmu 'alai-kum wa rahmanu 'Llāhi wa barakātu-Hu

Wa b'ad

Although, as you will no doubt be aware, I have often had news of you recently, I was extremely happy to hear from you directly, and also to hear that I may expect a visit from one of our friends; perhaps you yourself will be able to pay us a further visit before too long. . . .

Thank you for sending the successive chapters of your book, which has now been completed; I find it of the utmost interest, and it would have been a great pity if you had decided not to write it. There are no modifications that I could suggest, nor is there anything to add or delete; I think that what pertains to Christianity, in particular, has never before been presented from this point of view, and this may help some people to understand many things. It is important that this book should appear as soon as possible; Luc Benoist has told me that this might be towards the end of the year, but as the new edition of *The Crisis of the Modern World* will apparently come out sooner than he originally said, I hope that this may advance the publication of the succeeding volumes in the collection, that is to say: your book first, and then Coomaraswamy's [*Hinduism and Buddhism*]. As regards the new title for your book, it seems to me to be preferable to the earlier one, because it is shorter, and because it will perhaps also be clearer to readers who are not yet accustomed to our terminology.[1]

I had originally heard from P. Genty that he had decided to write you; I do not know what he has said to you on the subject of 'Prophets of the Spirit', but I am afraid that it will be something rather confused; he has unfortunately always been the same during the nearly 40 years that I have known him, and he is very stubborn in his ideas. . . . Clavelle, who told me that he had received a copy of your reply, says, following a more recent letter from Genty, that he 'seems adamant, now as before, not to leave his dream-world'; however, since Clavelle is not entirely free from prejudice in his regard, I would like to think that he exaggerates. If it really were true, it would be unfortunate for poor Genty, for it is indeed high time that he make a more 'effective' resolution'; he must now be 64 or 65 years old, but, to tell the truth, he has always seemed old. Regarding what you say in your reply about St John, there might be only this to add: many Muslims also consider St John to be a Prophet, belonging to the spiritual family of Al-Khidr, Sayyid-nā Idrīs, and Sayyid-nā Ilyas; but in any case, it is understood that he would only be *Nabī* and not *Rasūl*. In this connection, I do not recall if I ever had occasion to tell you that what gave me the idea to write the articles on 'descending realization' that were published at the beginning of 1939 was the fact that some Shi'ites claim that the *Walī* has a higher *maqām* (from the point of view of *al-qurb*, 'nearness') than the *Nabī* and even than the *Rasūl*. What I wrote recently about the *Malāmatīya*, as you will see (or perhaps already have seen, for the fourth number of *Études Traditionnelles* must now have appeared) also deals with the same question; this article agrees with what you yourself have written on the relationships between initiates and the people, and, by a curious coincidence(?), I

---

1. The original title proposed for Schuon's book (his first in French) was *De l'unité ésoterique des formes traditionnelles*. The title under which it finally appeared was *De l'unité transcendente des religions*. (Translator's note.)

had just conceived the idea to write it when this part of your book arrived!

Yes, I received from Buenos Aires the two studies which you mention on Buddhism and on the 'Divine Names'; I had the same impression of these, and especially of the latter, as you. It is very difficult to read and it contains many unnecessary complications, and even many correspondences that seem unjustified; I wonder on what authorities the author could base some of his assertions... Certainly the work of Abu Bakr [*The Book of Certainty*, by Martin Lings] is very different; don't you think that, if this were translated into French, it would be worth including in the collection *Tradition*? I do not think that Luc Benoist could have any objection to this idea.

I did indeed know Madame Breton (then Mademoiselle Dano) during my last days in Paris, and, since then, she has continued to write me from time to time. I think you did well to reply to her, for she is certainly very agreeable and seems to have a good understanding, and there is no reason not to have confidence in her; furthermore, it is a gratifying fact that she does not belong to that category of correspondents—all too numerous—who are troublesome and indiscrete. I should also mention that she and her brother-in-law (Paul Barbotin) were of considerable help to me in elucidating certain machinations of the 'R.I.S.S' and others of this kind. I will add, so that you know exactly what you are dealing with, that she is clearly Catholic, and that she is in touch with Charbonneau-Lassay.

Your chapter on the forms of art will certainly be most suitable for Bharata Iyer's volume [*Art and Thought*, a *Festschrift* in honor of Ananda Coomaraswamy's 70th birthday]; Marco Pallis wrote to say that he will prepare something on 'traditional dress'. As for myself, I have unfortunately done nothing so far; since it seems that the articles are required fairly soon, I wonder if a translation of my study on the theory of the elements, which appeared in the special number of *Études Traditionnelles* on the Hindu tradition, might not be suitable. It is in fact scarcely possible for me at the moment to write something of any length, nor will it be possible until I am completely finished with all questions concerning the publications and re-publications that are at present underway, for all of that takes up much time and is further complicated by the slowness and irregularity of the post. It is very true that the period of silence of these last years had several advantages for me, in the sense that otherwise it would probably have been difficult for me to succeed in completing 4 new books during this time; but, from another point of view, the prolonged absence of all news nevertheless became very hard. . . .

My thanks to you and all our friends for your good wishes; I continue in good health, praise be to God, and my family joins me in sending you our greetings and our happy memories.

Min al-faqīr ilā Rabbi-hi
'Abd al-Wāhid Yahyā

www.ingramcontent.com/pod-product-compliance
Lightning Source LLC
LaVergne TN
LVHW011412080426
835511LV00005B/497